Corporate
Capers

Corporate Capers

business *not* as usual

Dinesh Kumar

Response Books
A division of Sage Publications
New Delhi/Thousand Oaks/London

Copyright © Dinesh Kumar, 2006

First published in 2006 by

Response Books
A division of Sage Publications India Pvt Ltd
B-42, Panchsheel Enclave
New Delhi 110 017

Sage Publications Inc	Sage Publications Ltd
2455 Teller Road	1 Oliver's Yard
Thousand Oaks	55 City Road
California 91320	London EC1Y 1SP

Published by Tejeshwar Singh for Response Books, typeset in 10/12 pts. BruceOldStyle BT by Innovative Processors, New Delhi, and printed at Chaman Enterprises, New Delhi.

Library of Congress Cataloging-in-Publication Data

Kumar, Dinesh, 2 December 1937–
    Corporate capers:—business not as usual/Dinesh Kumar.
      p. cm.
    1. Leadership. 2. Industrial management. 3. Business ethics. I. Title.
HD57.7.K853 2005   658.4′092—dc22   2005024525

ISBN: 0–7619–3451–0 (Pb)   81–7829–598–9 (India–Pb)

Production Team: Leela Kirloskar, R.A.M. Brown, Ritu Singh and Santosh Rawat

Contents

7

C
O
N
T
E
N
T
S

This book is dedicated to all those starry-eyed students who dream of a wonderful corporate world led by corporate visionaries. It is also dedicated to middle managers, who have been the source of such valuable information on the lives and lore of their CEOs.

Leadership is not about what they taught you in your business schools. Leadership in the real corporate world is dynamically inconsistent, and full of surprises that keep you guessing and on your toes.

This book should help you to glide safely onto the runways of corporations instead of crash landing on them and ending up bruised.

Preface

CORPORATE CAPERS is a collection of short pieces, woven through the experience of 30 years in the corporate world. In these 30 years, I have had the honour of dealing with many CEOs, who were my role models in what leadership and management is made up of.

This book contains practical corporate philosophies and the doings of the golf-addicted, footloose, jet-set hyper-rich CEOs, who boast of private swimming pools, aircraft and gyms, financed by their companies, and whose stomachs enter the room before they do.

In this book, you will read about those 'enlightened' CEOs who sing the praises of Total Quality Management, as long as this collaborative style of management is not thrust upon *them*. Or, those who held forth on corporate governance but did not hesitate to have a battery of private companies through which all the buying and selling of the main company took place.

I am deeply indebted to the corporate sector, which provided me with all the raw material that I needed to make this book possible. No chef can assemble a gourmet meal without the right ingredients and the right environment. Luckily, the people mentioned, offered a plethora of opportunity.

Finally, any resemblance to any persons living or dead is absolutely intentional. If you are able to discern the characters, please feel free to write to me for a bumper prize... which may include a free lecture from that particular CEO!

August 2005   Dinesh Kumar

C
O
R
P
O
R
A
T
E

C
A
P
E
R
S

Acknowledgements

I'D LIKE to first say a hearty thank you to the CEOs I have met, worked with, and wined and dined. Without their fulsome, voluble, and often boastful narratives of their contributions to business and society, this book would never have been possible.

Thanks to the management of the *Deccan Herald*, Bangalore, and to Dilip Maitra, its Business Editor, who invited me to write the inside stories of the corporate world. These articles first made an appearance in the *Deccan Herald*, Bangalore.

Grateful thanks to Sadiqua Peerbhoy, a regular columnist, who, in the initial phases of my writing, taught me how to deal with the pink slips.

Finally, a big thank you to my wife, who usually has the last word in everything I say or write.

Part I

On Business Ethics (What's That?)

*Balance Sheet Botoxing** 1

A N IMPORTANT quality about consultants is that we are team players. It is said that even crooks have a code of conduct, like not transgressing one another's territory. Similarly, consultants also have their own code, as they need one another to get on in life, in a sort of win-win way.

For instance, if I am working with a client and he wants some financial botoxing done about which I do not know a sausage, I am hardly going to say no. 'Of course we can handle that', will be my answer. I know that I can always find an associate who will swing into action on my behalf, retaining 80 per cent of the fee and passing the rest to me for bringing him into the loop. That is how the system works. I suppose that is how the word *associate* consultant was coined.

One day, a long-forgotten client rang me and confided that he was sick.

I said, 'Why, what's wrong? Who are you seeing? I hope that it is nothing serious?'

Breaking into Hindi, he said, *'mein to bilkul theek hoon*. Company *ko* problem *hai'*.

That is how it is in India. They are always fine but their companies are not.

'What can I do for you, *bhai sahib*?' I asked, trying to sound helpful.

---

* Refers to a medical process by which wrinkles are reduced or removed

'*Ek* financial expert *ki zarurat hai*. I thought I would ask you.'

'When?' I asked.

'Emergency case *hai*.'

'No problem', I replied, mentally scanning for an associate to help. I thought of Gopal. I knew he could handle it. He was the best financial manicurist, pedicurist and facial expert, south of Vindyas. There was no financial wrinkle he could not botox out. He was that good. He helped one company to stay out of trouble for 10 whole years, before the financial institutions and banks could smell the proverbial rat. After doing that, he worked for the banks to make sure that the Reserve Bank of India (RBI) did not discover the existence of the dead rat! He is that smart. A wizard, really! But his fee is very steep.

Gopal's brief turned out to be the shortest he had ever received.

'Dress us so that no one knows we are naked.'

'Fine,' he said, and told the client that his services would have to be kept off the balance sheet. What a prudent fellow Gopal is! After the Arthur Anderson scandal, he wanted his association to be strictly off the record, and in cash.

So he gave the company a seven-fold recipe that kept them going for years. And before submitting it, as a matter of courtesy, he brought it to me to discuss.

'Give it to me in the KISS (Keep It Simple, Silly) form, Gopal', I said.

And tell me in a language even a school dropout can understand.

This is what he had to say:

It is obvious that this company needs to show that they are still solid and profitable, that they are cash rich and in the pink of health, whereas actually, they are deep in a financial quagmire.

This can be done in many ways but I will tell you the main ones in a language, that not only a school dropout but which even you can understand.

We call the first one the capitalising of revenue expenses.

I have to explain this to you in a way that you will easily understand. For instance, I know you like red wine. Yesterday, there was a report that red wine clears clogged arteries and, therefore, drinking it regularly is good for your heart. Understood? You have to drink it for a couple of years before you see any effect but the money on the wine has to be spent now.

In the same way, when you spend on advertisements, travel road shows, company literature, exhibitions and other marketing efforts, the money will be spent now but the benefits will take a lot of time to show. I am going to advise them to show only one-third of these expenses this year and charge the rest in the following years.

'Come on, sooner or later the chicks are going to go home to roost. Whom are they going to fool? You can't play the game forever!' I told him.

'I know. We will play it long enough till the banks catch up with the game and then I will hatch another plan', Gopal said.

'And then?'

'They will be a part of the problem and become partners in solving it.' Gopal said.

I did not want to know more but he insisted on continuing his lesson.

The second one is on inventory management.

'Now, supposing you want to get your daughter married though you are broke but you want to grab the attention of this non-resident Indian (NRI) guy, what would you do?' he asked.

'How on earth do I know? My children got married and sent me copies of the certificates of their marriages for an ipso facto sanction!' I told him impatiently.

'You are lucky but what you would do is to borrow some expensive household goods, some furniture, some paintings, an additional TV set, and a car from your friends, to make your home look complete. You can fill Indian whisky in scotch bottles. All these props will ensure that you'll look wealthy. So, now you have a rich son-in law and by the time he discovers your true state and asks for a divorce, he will have to pay alimony to your daughter. Or, if he sticks with your daughter, he will have to also maintain you. Like the banks, he will become a part of the problem!'

'We apply the same principal here. We have no stock but on paper, it exists. We have half-finished goods but we declare them to be "finished". We have fridge boxes with neither motors nor compressors, but we show them as complete, ready to sell stocks. And we can hock them for more and more loans and show potential profit.' By now, he was out of breath and asked for a glass of water.

When I suggested a beer, he said that he had only 'clean habits'. And a dirty scheming mind, I wanted to add.

'There is more if you want to hear...' He could see that my attention span on these matters was limited.

'But before you go any further, what about the auditors? The watch dogs will sniff your scheme out sooner than you think!' I exclaimed.

'They gave us no problems even earlier but now you can get hordes of them at half the cost from the

US. I work with them. They are willing to overlook things', he said, sounding confident.

'What else are you advising them?' I asked.

'The third wrinkle-free scheme you will find difficult to understand but I will try,' said Gopal.

'Say, if people òwe you Rs 50 million and you show that they owed you Rs 80 million. And suppose you owe people Rs 50 million but showed that you owed them only Rs 30 million. You have done Rs 50 million of botoxing! Here, of course, we will be doing it on a much bigger scale.'

'That is taking the game too far. That is nothing but outright fudging of figures!' I was livid at his suggestion. 'I wouldn't let you send this proposal on my letterhead,' I said firmly.

'I am just making a proposal. The fudging will be done by the client. I will only provide the tools of how to issue credit and debit notes. Remember, I told you my work is off the balance sheet and so are my payments.'

'The fourth suggestion I have is....'

I stopped him, 'Enough, Gopal. I want to sleep on the pillow of clear conscience; and remind me to do something about my personal portfolio, which is in a mess.' Having said that, I let out a yawn over a mile long, a signal he never fails to miss.

I carried my cognac to the bedroom, as is my wont.

Bhai sahib rang me, some months later, to thank me for Gopal's services.

Greed for Gadgetry 2

A N ASSOCIATE consultant I work with, is a Sherlock Holmes in financial matters. He can sniff a whiff of financial wrongdoing or laxity from a distance of one kilometre. He has even picked up the habit of saying, 'Elementary, my dear Dinesh!'

He and I complement each other perfectly, for my knowledge of financial matters would not cover a one-rupee coin and he cannot navigate his way through the meandering managerial maze.

Some time ago, a leading bank asked us to study a company on the brink of closure. Our brief was short:

'Go forth, foot soldiers and find the demon that destroyed a jewel of a company,' said the chairman.

My job was over in a day because the company did not have any management procedures at all, written or otherwise. Though there were departments for different functions with heads of departments (with impressive designations), they were mere note takers and highly paid ones at that! All decisions went right up to the thirteenth floor. I knew I did not have much to do except to write a 25-page evaluation (anything less would not do to claim the fee) for the bank. So, most of the time I tagged along with my friend and regarded the tour of the company's financials as an education.

What we discovered during the course of discussions with the management was incredible. My friend found that it was not the competition, or the recession in the market which caused the rot: it was the CEO's obsession with gadgetry!

If he saw something new in the market, he had to buy it immediately, whatever the cost. Like the golf club with Tiger Wood's monogram. He just had to own the latest laptop (although he needed someone else for sending and receiving his emails), the latest mobile phone, and other fancy electronic personal gadgets. Then, when he got bored with these toys, he would pass them on to his friends and family and upgrade to the newer, sleeker, models. Between winks of sleep, I would hear the dialogue between my friend and the heads of departments.

'If he sees a CNC machine in a trade fair anywhere in the world, he must have it, whether we need it or not. We have more CNC machines in our company than all the competition put together', said the VP, production.

'I want to see your capital equipment procurement procedures', demanded the financial whiz kid.

'We have none.' came the reply.

'I don't believe that,' said the shocked Sherlock.

'It's true!' was the response.

'Holy cow!' said the detective.

'What?' I asked.

'Forget it,' he mumbled.

'We are just informed of what has been ordered. I remember a Japanese delegation visiting us and the leader, at the end of the visit, said that we must be a cash-rich company,' said the VP sadly. 'If only he knew . . . !'

At this stage, another colleague took over. He said, 'If only the Japs knew that we are not cash rich, we are cash strapped! We just borrow heavily to meet the CEO's tech-spree expenses'.

'But surely, you would have brought this to the notice of the boss man?' My colleague was getting impatient. 'Surely, *someone* would have gone through the normal procedures of first establishing the need?'

'We usually found out about the purchase after it was done, and when we did point that out, we were branded as a bunch of conservatives,' moaned the production chief.

He continued, 'Once I made a presentation, giving facts and figures, to establish that we had built and were still building, in capacities to a level that could meet the entire country's need. I asked in desperation whether we were going to wipe out all the competition from the face of the country.'

'What was the response?' asked my friend.

'He called the marketing chief to tell him to push up the top line to get the ratios right.'

It appeared that the marketing man was the only person who knew how to handle the boss. He would hear him out, neither agree or disagree, and then go and do what he thought was right.

'Can you believe that?' asked my friend, looking at me in disbelief.

'I believe everything about companies. Unlike you, I don't want to raise my blood pressure,' I answered.

The finance manager said that he had informed the chief of how the interest-to-sales ratio was mounting at an alarming rate and that company sales could just not support the mindless expansion.

Over lunch, we heard more horror stories. Of how a private jet was bought to take the chief and all his top managers to Delhi in one hop. It did not matter that the city was connected to the capital by seven commercial flights. I also learnt that the annual cost of owning an aircraft through interest, hangarage and a crew was Rs 20 million.

'And you know what, we still haven't seen the inside of the aircraft because *we* have to take the commercial flights for our travel . . . !' complained one of them.

The next day was no different. This time we visited the capital purchase manager, who had a sense of humour and said that he needed it to cope with the madness.

'Who told you that I am the capital purchase chief?' He laughed. 'I'm the capital purchase regularisation clerk and the highest paid clerk in the world!' He adjusted his tie in mock importance. His job was to complete the formality for audit purposes and to ensure that the chief signed all requisitions.

I liked this rotund gentleman, who laughed as he told us several anecdotes of reckless purchases. 'One day a group of people walked in to say that they were here to network the entire company, the dealers, the suppliers and the sales offices.'

My friend listened with rapt attention.

'So, we invested in a state-of-the-art computer network system. We paid Rs 170 million for it. The idea was that in a jiffy, any one of our suppliers, dealers, branch offices and departments could enter the system and receive updates before taking any decision. Now it is one big box on my table,' he said pointing to a covered computer terminal.

'The joke is that we did not have the manual systems in place to transfer data on to the computer. And computers demand transparency. But secrecy is the name of the game here.'

My friend was baffled. 'Don't tell me that there is no control structure in your company? Surely, there is a Board to ask questions and approve capital expenses? Don't you need Board approval for all big purchases?' he asked.

'Sir *ji*, Board *hai*. *Par* captive Board *hai*. Once, I built up the courage to confide in the bank nominee director. He asked me for all the details. Though I gave them to him, nothing happened. I felt like an idiot.'

'The best part is, that the fellow has got a foreign posting with the IMF.' He laughed his guts out, as if he was enjoying himself giving us the low down.

'My real job is to hold mock negotiations with vendors who will never get the order,' said the corporate clerk.

'Why?' asked my colleague.

'Because minutes after my meeting, the winning vendor and the boss will be shaking hands.' He extended his hand as if to demonstrate.

We'd learned everything there was to know. My friend couldn't stop shaking his head. Time to go, we knew. So, I asked my friend to make the pre-departure call on the chief because I was feeling hot under the collar and wanted a beer badly.

My friend, being a finance man, does not touch any hard liquor. His favourite drink is soda on soda with lots of ice. Writing reports is thirsty work.

Big Chiefs' Appetites 3

GOING BY the global consumption of CEOs, whatever you put in their plates is chicken feed. I refer here to the insatiable appetite of corporate generals for pay and perquisites.

You may recall how the champions of the Indian industry did everything possible in the early stages of liberalisation to thwart the pace of reforms. They showed stiff resistance to change every step of the way. Remember the Club that existed in Bombay? According to the corporate grapevine, meetings are not held any more due to the lack of interest of its members and the inability to have a quorum.

These chieftains used to argue that the Indian industry needs more time to organise itself to face global competition. Having lived in the licence-permit raj for over four decades, it was not fair to expose us to competition so quickly, the industrialists argued. *Give us a level playing field on the interest rates and on labour reforms*, they clamoured. *Improve the infrastructure to global levels before globalisation; calibrate the response to globalisation;* and *give us access to international finance*, they demanded of the government.

The industry was being cajoled out of its cosy quilt of protection. Its leaders were discovering that not only was the temperature outside too cold for comfort but they also had to make an early start in the morning and return home very late, unlike the good old days. Competition can do some crazy things to business people. It can rob them of their sleep and happiness.

However, the one change the industrialists happily took to, as the proverbial fish takes to the water, was the liberalisation of their pay and perquisites. Every AGM's first resolution was to pass hefty increases in the emoluments of their CEOs, within days of the upper limits being lifted. Some could not even wait for the next AGM and convened EGMs to pass pay package increases, which hit the roof. These changes were so sudden, that the shareholders were treated with total disdain. The Boards were packed with the cronies of the CEOs, and the directors, in their mutual interest, who were willing to nod their heads even before the last word on the resolution had been spoken. We must surely hold the dubious distinction of the record number of resolutions, unanimously passed by the Board. Who chooses the Board anyway? In effect, it is the CEO and the board members are beholden to him.

'Tough times make CEOs costlier', I recently read this headline in one of the business dailies. The figures of salaries and perks mentioned were in the range of Rs 10–12 million per annum. Many will say that I am being judgemental if I term these figures obscene. You make your call at the end of this chapter. They are obscene because they are totally discordant with and out of proportion to the wages the engineers or workers of the company get. An engineer's salary per annum may be Rs 200,000–250,000 and workers may have to settle for Rs 50,000–60,000. A decent society must have decent norms. Would you call it decent if the salary of the CEO were 500 times more than that of an engineer, and 2000 times that of a worker? They are obscene not only in relative terms but also in absolute terms. And I am no socialist.

I understand that there are arguments galore that heatedly debate the salaries of CEOs in the US. They quote the recent case of the head of the New York Exchange, who signed for himself a package so extravagant, that he had to quit in shame. Talk of mis-governance and the case of Enron is thrown at you. Talk about the US action in Iraq and you will hear that the US had no business to invade a sovereign state. A case of selective role modelling, some would say. As an aside, you should know that corporate India is very peeved at being asked to open their bags at American airports for security reasons. *Do you know who I am?* does not work there. That you should respect the laws of the country you are visiting is soon forgotten.

If you talk of Narayan Murthy and his modest salary, the response you will get is that with the kind of shareholding he has, he can afford to be modest about his salary. They make it sound as if the shareholding has come to him as a gift from heaven. Talk to them about Azim Premji's frugal style and they will label it as a case of inverted snobbery. Anything or any means will do, to justify and protect their cosy position.

There was a little item in the newspaper recently about the government's intention of raising the directors' sitting fees to attract independent directors. It would be a mistake because the ability of a director to open his mouth in disagreement is inversely proportional to the money he is going to get. Aren't there any passionate leaders available, who will speak on behalf of minority shareholders without carrots hanging in front of them?

Have a heart, some would say. You don't want the government to get involved in our salary structure again, do you? It is precisely for this reason that I argue that the industry needs to display some self-restraint before this gross disparity becomes an issue within organisations, and between the industry and the government. It would be unwise to think that when the workers and middle management see such a patent disparity between what they get and what their bosses get, they will accept the situation smilingly as a part of the capitalist society structure. You can be sure there will be heartburn leading to strife within the organisations and the society. Another certainty is that it will lead to corruption within organisations. Experience tells us that what people can't set right by fair means, they achieve by foul ones.

Workers and middle managers will ask and rightly so, what kind of meat do the CEOs eat that they need such high wages to live, while we get so little in comparison? Are they the only value creators in the companies? Does the market cap of the companies depend only on them? Where do they think the companies would be without our contribution?

It will be an enlightened leadership that asks itself whether it is not obscene to drive into the company in a Rs 20 million Bentley, when our workers are still riding bicycles.

It would be foolish to think that this obscene disparity will not create a chasm between the workers and the management.

Whether industry associations ever discuss these issues or whether they are too uncomfortable to be raised in their forum, is a question to be asked and answered. It is possible that they believe, in this respect at least, we are at par with the rest of the world. However, it must be these associations that should call for a review because neither the government nor the SEBI should be involved. The restraint should come from within.

Let us remember that capitalism and concern for the underdog are not mutually exclusive. Capitalism can only survive in a sphere of harmony. A re-look at the salary structure will be in the self-enlightened interest of the industry.

How to Conduct an AGM 4

IF THERE was one company that I wanted to quit as soon as I joined, it was this one. My contractual obligations, however, demanded that I serve at least one year. So, I stayed from one AGM to the next, give or take a few hours.

This company regarded its AGMs very seriously. The preparation for the annual event was done under the able leadership of the company secretary, who was a bit of a crook (and a crook with some knowledge of the law can be a deadly combination).

The chairman of the Board suffered no fools, and here, it appeared that he had a whole lot of them attending the AGM, reflecting on important issues like executive pays and perks, expenses on foreign travel and other business of the company, as if they owned it (if people only knew what this guy thought of shareholders…).

The chairman was usually so badly stressed out after an AGM, that he would take the first flight to Thailand to de-stress. Company gossip had it that an hour of body massage in an exclusive parlour did wonders to his psyche.

Pam, his PR manager, who fluttered her eyes and, who was known to be more capable behind a filing cabinet than in front of it, always accompanied him. For the boss in this company, PR meant Personal Relations and he flourished in personal relations with this special perquisite, which was exclusively his. But this chapter is neither about the chairman, nor Pam and not even that crook, the company secretary.

I happened to be present on one occasion when the company secretary and the VP finance briefed the chairman about the AGM preparation.

'How is it going? I don't want a repeat of a situation when some idiot or the other from Palampur once again asks the expenses incurred on my foreign travel to be published separately. I have a feeling someone from your department is leaking information to them.' He looked at the finance man accusingly.

'It is all under control' This was that crook, the company secretary. 'That man will be singing your praises. All I had to do was to post his son, who works in our dispatch department, to our Gauhati office.'

'That is the way to deal with some of these fellows.' the boss intoned.

'He was on his knees. I have given him the gist of what he has to say.' The legal man continued with his briefing. 'And what is that? the boss man asked.

'That without your able leadership, the company would have been referred to the BIFR. By the way, I have told him to wear a blue shirt so that you can recognise him and acknowledge him when he raises his hand.'

'What else?'

The finance man, not to be outdone, mentioned what he had done to help. He said that he had released money from the scrap sale cash to the company secretary to buy some favours for the regular troubleshooters.

'I called all those jokers who stand up to show off their knowledge of the balance sheet and cut deals with them. This time there will be no problem. I will whisper the colour of their shirts so that you can recognise them to say their bit and not others.'

'We have thought of another strategy', continued the wily finance man. 'I was telling Lakshman', looking at the legal man, 'that we should serve the refreshments sometime after our *own* shareholders have made speeches. So, when it is time to move the resolution, there will be very few people left.'

'A very good idea,' said the chairman, 'because half of them come to the AGMs for bread *pakodas* anyway. Why the hell do you have these fellows complain of bad quality *gulab jamun*? Give them something good and get rid of them.'

'We will do that', both said, trying to please the *sahib*.

The chairperson tried to involve me in the discussion since I was sitting as still and quiet as a duck, absorbing this fantastic conversation.

'You have any ideas?'

'Not really! I will stick to the role of giving you the explanatory notes needed. Remember, someone asked you whether we followed the straight line or the written down method of depreciation and you had some difficulty then. The only thing that I might add is that when you recognise the shareholder, it will be nice if you said, "you sir, in the third row". I think that *sir* would sit well with them.'

'I know old chap. You were a great help last time'', he said in acknowledgement, of making him look less foolish than he was at the last AGM. I was surprised that I, a raw hand from the airforce, knew more about assets and liabilities than this chap did. He did not know why the assets had to be balanced with the liabilities.

'Another thing that we have done is to fix the meeting at 9 a.m. so that it is too early for most people to reach the venue'. This was the VP, finance.

'By the way, where is the meeting anyway?' I asked.

'This time we have fixed it up in a hotel near Hosur, a bit out of the way, though.'

'Yes, good idea. The fewer people the better', said the chairman

I had some difficulty suppressing a smile because just the previous day he had finalised our mission statement, which said *that our shareholders are our owners. They provide us the capital and it will be our endeavour to do our utmost to enhance the shareholders' value.* Pam, the HR manager, was beside herself writing the script. Poor girl, if only she knew something other than the physical side of her boss.

'But there is one guy who has been coming year after year, that retired accountant, who asks tricky questions on deferred revenue expenses and capitalising revenue expenses. Frankly, he is the one who puts me off, for I don't know what to tell him.'

The finance man kept quiet out of politeness because he knew that he had covered the ground on this point already. Besides, he did not want the boss to know the little games he played to make the balance sheet look good.

'By the way, where have you arranged the lunch after the meeting. Is there any place where you can get fresh seafood like crabs and prawns? We want to do the best for our directors, don't we?'

'Lunch is at the new place on MG road where they serve fresh seafood. I believe they have imported a chef from France. And their barman is known to mix the best dry martinis in town. We have booked a foursome slot at the golf course for you and other golfing directors.' This was the legal guy.

'This man from the financial institution is getting on my nerves. He is turning out to be some sort of freeloader. Last time it was a holiday in Ooty with the family. This time he wants to go to Kodai', complained the chairman.

'*Rehne do saar*, he is a great help in the restructuring plan of our company. He also gives me a lot of tips on how to make the minutes of the AGM in a manner acceptable to the financial institutions. He has asked me to join him in the trip to Kodai,' piped in the finance man.

'By the way, have you fixed up the names of all those who will propose and second the resolutions?'

'Yes sir. I have also told the seconders to wait until the proposers have finished. Remember last time some eager beavers got up even before the proposers had moved the resolutions.'

With all the weighty matters concluded, the chairman closed the meeting and the two left the room without realising that I was right behind them.

The con man was thanking his buddy from finance for all the help, to which he replied.

'*Yehi to hai* team work, *bandhu*'.

I knew what I had to do after the AGM.

Post script: The AGM went off without a hitch.

All the proposals went through with resounding yes's.

The legal man received a fast-track promotion.

The finance man got a trip abroad to visit his son.

And the chairman got my resignation letter.

The Board Meets Before it Actually Meets 5

THERE IS something special about the word 'Boardroom'. This hallowed portal of corporate power means different things to different people. For some, the word sends shivers down their spines. For others, it generates respect and reverence.

On the day of the Board meeting, employees either avoid taking the route adjacent to the Boardroom, or walk past it with their heads bowed in deference.

Why does this room, which like any other, has a large table, about a dozen odd chairs, a few carpets, and a couple of paintings, evoke such an intense response?

It is because they believe that it is in this room, that the destiny of the company is determined. It is here that strategic decisions are taken. It is here that their futures are shaped. After all, is it not here that the vast, specialised, and combined expertise of directors in finance, marketing, human relations, and company law is brought to bear upon weighty corporate issues?

This room is where the chairman chairs the meetings. From this room, decisions travel to the AGMs and to the shareholders (the real owners) to ratify.

It is next to this room that gleaming cars are parked by the directors' white uniformed chauffeurs, every three months. It will be from this room that they will be whisked away for lunch to a seven-star retreat after the meeting is over. So, no wonder the boardroom is important and has an aura around it, even when the lights are off and the room is empty.

The facts may be somewhat different.

The Board meets before it actually meets. In fact, usually an hour or two before it is due to meet—in the CEO's vast office for consensus building on issues connected with the company and its directors.

It is here that they troop in one by one. And the first question as they enter is likely to be:

'So what are we discussing today?'

It could quite possibly be that some of them have actually read a part of the agenda on the way to the meeting. It could also be that some may have forgotten to carry their papers and will ask for a spare copy on arrival. A few others may be depending on an oral briefing in an abridged form from the CEO, as a part of the consensus-building exercise. 'He is going to tell us anyway', is their time-saving logic.

You see, in the Boardroom, there will be company employees like VPs present; all the functionaries. That is no place to show any difference in opinion, ignorance of subject, or lack of preparation!

And with some consensus already built, you can reduce the time of the official meeting. Also, you can finish formalities like signing the attendance register, collecting the sitting fee, and actual expenses. Why have the assistant secretary and cashier intrude into the formal meeting and dish out money in full view of all and sundry? It does not look nice.

Well, the CEO will respond to the directors before the start of the meeting, 'Let all of them come and then we can informally go over the agenda.'

One would think that is a lot of time wasted but no, it is time well spent. How? For example, my grandnephew has done his MBA from an unrecognised school of management in Tumkur; so I might take the CEO to the north-east corner of his room and say:

I wanted to talk to you about this little matter about my grandnephew who has just done his MBA. I thought if he started his career in our company under your watchful eyes and able guidance, his foundation would become solid. You know how youngsters are these days? Money is not an issue, whether he gets any pay or not. He comes from a good family—my family. It is experience, good, solid experience the boy is looking for.

This little conversation is making others in the room uncomfortable on two counts. First, they are thinking *I hope there will be some time left for me*, and second, *I hope that fellow is not talking about the issue I wanted to discuss. Oh, good, they have finished!* And now the second director catches the CEO's eyes and takes him to the south-west corner for a little pow-wow, which might go something like this:

I just wanted to tell you that my travel has considerably reduced. I do have some spare time. The new sub committees on audit, corporate governance, and the company's future plans are due to be reconstituted after the AGM. I thought that I would mention to you that I would be quite happy to serve on one or two of them. That way I will be also able to keep in touch with you.

At this stage the CEO might slip in a suggestion: *Ah, that reminds me. I wanted to talk to you about something. I thought that the Education Trust we have, if my wife was looking after it as its Chief Trustee, I will be able to monitor it closely.*

To which the co-director will respond: *I think it is a good idea. I don't mind moving the resolution when the chair asks for any other point.*

There are various other important matters like these that need to be resolved. They could range from a trip abroad, finding suitable jobs for relatives and an extra perk here and there, to putting in a word to that government official the CEO knows and you don't (where one of your files is stuck at his table for a decision). There are many issues in this complicated world and these need a collaborative effort to solve.

'So, what are we discussing today', asks a director who is the last to arrive.

So, the consensus building on the company matters start and the first point on the agenda is the issue of the CEO's pay and perks. And he dismisses the whole thing with a flourish of his hand that all that is given there is within government guidelines. The consensus builds without a hitch because in any case, they are within the government guidelines. It does not violate any corporate governance guidelines (which are a different matter entirely).

'And the second point on the agenda is....'

At this stage, most likely, the assistant secretary enters and announces that it is time for the meeting and that everyone has arrived.

'Tell them we will join them in five minutes', says the CEO.

In those precious five minutes, the CEO goes through the pros of the points contained in the agenda. There is no time to mention the cons. They are waiting, aren't they?

'In any case you can tell us there', says the non-executive chairman.

The directors enter the portal of power—the Boardroom. The assistant secretary keeps the door open to allow them to walk in. The functionaries get up and become serious all at once. The assistant secretary pulls out the chair ceremoniously and the official meeting is brought to order by the non-executive chairman.

The Seven Habits of Highly Perfidious People

ORPORATE GOVERNANCE is the latest buzzword being tossed around. You never know—in the (very) distant future, ethical and value-based governance might actually become a reality in India! In the meanwhile, till the good times last, I list below the highly effective and time-tested ways of making money while governing corporations. If you get the hang of all of them, there is one person who will probably be very proud of you—Stephen Covey—author of *The Seven Habits of Highly Effective People*.

Habit 1: During the Planning Phase

You want to own the majority holding in your new project during the start-up phase. If the initial equity capital is Rs 10 crore, you will be required to arrange a little over 5 crore to retain 51 per cent ownership. With companies facing many hostile takeovers these days, you don't want *(a)* to leave anything to chance; or *(b)* your hard work to go down the drain. Go ahead and decide on a mark-up on the land and capital machinery purchases. Make sure you personally negotiate all large purchases. With these simple precautions, you will easily recover the entire investment during the construction phase itself. You will also have absolute control without putting in a single *paisa* from your pocket. With nothing at stake, you can enjoy a peaceful, uninterrupted sleep!

Habit 2: Operations Begin

The minister of state for industry inaugurates your factory. During his speech he congratulates you for being an entrepreneur and calls you a visionary (which you are—you envision your large personal wealth!) and for the job opportunities you have created. Soon after that, set up a few private limited companies ensuring that they are controlled by your immediate family. These companies can be entrusted with the raw material purchases. You don't want to be messing around with too many vendors, as Total Quality Management (TQM) has taught you that variety in vendors is the enemy number one of quality. You'll find that there is also less paperwork when you are dealing with fewer vendors. While you are at it, ensure that any scrap sale is directly controlled by you. Since most scrap dealers like paying by cash—you certainly don't want it falling in the wrong hands!

Habit 3: During Sales

You are about to celebrate the marriage of your son, which, keeping in view your lofty position, must be celebrated with pomp and splendour. You will need to invite all your customers, as well as numerous industry leaders. No problem at all! Tell your dealers and buyers that you have to urgently pay some money to a political leader. They will be more than happy to hand over the necessary cash. They will also place very large orders with your company. You can then compensate them with an additional discount under the guise of the highly competitive prevailing market conditions. Do consider routing some of your sales through these private limited companies. It will be to your benefit in more ways than one!

Habit 4: Modernisation

You don't want to be left behind in today's globally wired world. The latest technology will help you to stay ahead of the competition. So, make sure you choose the best that is available—don't skimp on the expenses! Plan for the next 10 years. Think big—the greater the expense, the larger the opportunity in absolute terms—even if the mark-up is constant. Remember, overseas purchases render dollar opportunities in their wake. . .

Habit 5: Set Up a Trust

Set up an educational trust in your grandfather's name, which will endorse his humble beginnings, as well as yours. Make sure you are appointed its chief trustee and get the board to approve some funding for a noble cause. Contributions can also be tax free. Now you can send your son abroad for higher learning and let the trust take care of the expenses...

Habit 6: Controlling Personal Expenses

As a corporate person, you know the importance of the top line, which you have already taken care of. You are also aware that expense control is equally important for a healthy bottom line. My next suggestion comes in handy here. Corporate club memberships! Become a member of as many clubs as you can. Charge all entertainment expenses to the company. Set up a gym in your factory, and order one extra treadmill for your personal use. If anyone asks, tell them it helps improve your mind–body connection.

Habit 7: During Restructuring

TQM has taught you that the quality of your products and services depends on the quality of the processes involved in producing them. So, you are more than aware that with the suggestions given above, the company will eventually become financially 'sick'. Start capitalising your revenue expenses, overvaluing the inventory and using other standard procedures which are termed 'window dressings'. You are a leader—leaders view problems as opportunities.

By the time bankers and financial institutions discover what you are up to, it will be too late for them to do anything. They will be all too aware that they have been caught napping. Since they don't want to have additional non-paying asset woes on their plate, they will help you to create a restructuring plan for the purpose of submitting to an appropriate court of law, which will be eventually accepted. It will most likely include selling off the company's assets to pay off its debts. One more opportunity to make some money! In any event, your stake at this point is zero (see Habit 1).

If you are a novice at the game of good corporate governance, you might be worried about the auditor. Don't worry. Remember, who appoints the auditors? Your Board of Directors! If you recall, these include board members who cup their ears to hear the conversation during the Board meetings; who require a pair of magnifying glasses to read the agenda papers; and who excelled in unsavoury education. They will, therefore, completely understand your compulsions.

Do remember to frequently mention the continued demands your friendly politicians and civil servants keep making to you. Attend the auditor's daughter's wedding and present her with an expensive gift. Do make it a point also to attend industry association meetings for more tips on corporate governance. Ask your company secretary to prepare a paper on the subject, so that you can read it out at the meeting.

This is, of course, only theory. In the end, theory will take you this far and no further. For practical training, look for a role model to learn how he puts these seven habits into practice to become a highly perfidious person, and success will be yours!

Converting Butter Chicken into a Tot of Rum 7

I F YOU think that it is only the Government of India that makes inane rules and regulations that cannot be enforced, you're wrong. Companies all over the world do exactly the same thing and feel very good about it. Often the stupidity index of the rules is directly proportional to the size of the company. The bigger the company, the greater the number of unenforceable rules.

I have this habit of chatting with drivers, engineers and managers when I am with them. It is often from these conversations that I get insights into the functioning of their companies. Sometimes, I think that I should share my fee with them, for without their help, where would I get the ideas for writing these articles? (But then, what I get for writing just about takes me as far as a Bacardi bottle and that is one thing that I will share over my dead body).

Well, one day, I was travelling from Bangalore to Delhi and happened to be sitting next to a risen from-the-ranks servicing manager—a Bihari gentleman in his mid-forties.

'What are travel rules like in your company?', I asked. 'I mean, how do you decide which hotel you can stay and how much you can spend on taxis and food and other needs?'

'*Saale paagal hain* rule *banane wale*. These rule makers are mad. *Unko* vouchers *chahiye, aur kuchh nahin*. They need vouchers and nothing else.'

With just a bit of prodding I heard the whole story.

'You see, our company has two pages of rules on food and beverages. They say that for all three meals, we will be allowed a certain amount. Also, we can spend the money only for food. Drinks are our personal expenditures.'

'So, you have to get separate bills for food and for liquor?' I inquired.

'Nothing like that. We sign vouchers for food for the upper limit. I don't eat breakfast but I sign the voucher for it. Lunch is usually eaten in the company we are visiting. But we sign the voucher for lunch as well.'

'What do you mean *we?*' I asked, to clarify.

'Everyone.'

'You mean everyone in your company does that?' I asked in mock surprise.

'Everyone and every company, *ji.*'

'Don't tell me the hotels are willing to give you vouchers for food when you don't eat there?' I persisted.

He looked at me as if I were mentally challenged, an assessment my wife would have heartily shared if she were a part of the conversation.

'*Unka kya jata hai*. In the evening when we want a drink, they give it to us.'

I understood from him that the common joke in their company was *dal makhani ko* rum *banaana*. Converting *dal* into rum.

'Sometimes we have dinner with our relatives. *Woh bhi* included for drinks shrinks.' He continued. '*Saale paagal hai*, these finance people. They should just set the upper limit. Their work will be less or *hum ko* game *khelna nahin padega*.'

'I wonder why companies make rules that cannot be enforced?' I asked.

'I said, *na*. They are mad. Same thing with the taxis. Voucher *lao*. I can go by an auto-rickshaw and get a voucher for a taxi.

I thought that the man was right. Why make a rule that cannot be enforced, that encourages your people into cheating the company?

My friend was in a talkative mood, so he carried on.

'Tell me sir, if I am on a service job, can anyone check whether I have planned my route or whether I am crisscrossing the city from one call to another. If they trust me to do a good job there, why do they want vouchers for my food bill?'

'Then what is the solution?' I asked.

'It is simple. *Yeh tumhara* food *ka* allowance *hai*. *Jo karna hai karo*. Whether I have chicken or rum, if I don't exceed the upper limit, what is your problem?'

Frankly, I empathised with the man. In my own time, I had seen so many unenforceable rules and yet, we lived with them year after year. I once worked for a company in which we were put on probation for six months after each promotion. My status changed from an employee to a probationer six times, so on each promotion, from a confirmed employee I became a probationer for six months. My employees were checking on my ability to perform my new job responsibilities.

If my performance as general manager was not satisfactory, I could be demoted, the company secretary told me, hesitatingly. Then he told me that even government departments have the same rule. *What makes you think you are so special that even rules similar to the government ones don't apply to you?*

I knew it was time to beat a hasty retreat, fearing that he might summarily extend my probationary period.

I asked him how many employees had been demoted under this clause. 'In my, er, memory, no one so far.'

I must confess that when I climbed the corporate ladder and became a part of the policy-making group, I still didn't do anything to modify it.

You see, we had all served with that clause, so what was the harm in continuing it? We agreed unanimously.

When lunch was over, I asked whether there was any other rule he thought was unnecessary. He thought hard, then said, '*Ek aur* rule *hai*, which is very difficult to enforce.'

'Which is that?' I sought.

'*Yeh* bonds *ka* rule. When you go for a course abroad, you have to sign a bond for some years. *Main to* abroad *nahin gaya* but some of my colleagues left the company before the bond period was over. Not one recovery was made.'

'Not even one?' I asked, incredulously.

'*Saare* court case *ban gaye.*'

I was taken aback by that statement, when I remembered that the situation was no different in our company.

When I dug deeper, I discovered that the origin of these rules was audit objections. One infringement, one objection, one rule, followed by infringement of that rule, covered by another rule. The rules were made to satisfy the auditors and not made from the point of view of functionality.

It is the same with the contracts signed with the employee. There are only a couple of clauses that are worthwhile in the contracts that I have seen. Mainly, it is the one connected with separation and the notice period.

My friend woke up after a snooze, yawned and said he would not be surprised if his company came with one more unenforceable rule. 'Like what?' I asked.

'Something like, "with immediate effect any employee contracting a transmittable disease will report of this occurrence to the company through proper channels."' He laughed.

'And get an acknowledgement from his superior for having reported it', I spiced it up.

He broke into a big guffaw.

I dropped him at his hotel on the way to mine and thought to myself that the journey must have at least been worth two bottles in taxi fare. He asked me for my card and said, '*Thoda zyada hi bol diya*. I talked a bit too much.' I winked at him and said:

'Singh *sahib, iss hamam mein sab nange hein*. We are all naked in the same bath tub.' We shook hands as we parted.

Corporate Conformance 8

When two people in business always agree, one of them is unnecessary.

—William Wrigley

I RECEIVED an email recently with this quote that so succinctly describes the monkey-like behaviour in the corporate sector. Some of you may have heard the following story before but it is worth repeating here:

> Put eight monkeys together in a room. In the centre of the room is a ladder, leading to a bunch of bananas that are hanging from a hook on the ceiling. Each time a monkey tries to climb the ladder, all the monkeys are sprayed with ice water. This thwarts their attempts and also makes them wet, cold, and miserable.
>
> Soon it is observed that whenever a monkey tries to climb the ladder, all of the other monkeys, not wanting to be sprayed, set upon him and beat him up. Very soon, none of the eight monkeys go near the ladder.
>
> After a while, one of the original monkeys is removed from the room and a new monkey is brought in. Seeing the bananas and the ladder, he wonders why none of the other monkeys is doing the obvious. Undaunted, he immediately begins to climb the ladder. All the other monkeys fall upon him and beat him silly. He has no idea why, however, he no longer attempts to climb the ladder.
>
> A second original monkey is removed and replaced. The newcomer again attempts to climb the ladder but all the other monkeys proceed to hammer him. This includes the first new replacement monkey, who, grateful that he is not at the receiving end this time, participates in the beating because all the other monkeys are doing it. However, he has no idea why he is attacking the new monkey.
>
> One by one, all the original monkeys are replaced. Now there are eight new monkeys in the room. None of them has ever been sprayed by the ice water. None of them attempts to climb the ladder. All of them will enthusiastically beat up any new monkey who tries to climb it, without having any idea why.

I couldn't have found a better example to describe exactly the same type of behaviour in the corporate sector.

Recently, being a member of a non-governmental organisation (NGO) I attended a workshop organised by an NGO. When the chairperson of the organisation said, that for the NGO to be effective, they needed 'like-minded people', he could have quite easily said, 'like-minded and obeying monkeys'.

Conformity is the name of the game and conformity translates itself into averageness. Preserving a structure is more important than accepting another paradigm. *We have always done it this way. This is our philosophy. Either you believe in it or you don't. Either you are with us or you are with the enemy.*

Recently, the CEO of a fast-moving consumer goods (FMCG) company was in the news, having been asked to leave in somewhat murky circumstances. I asked an industrialist what was his take on the reason of this hasty exit. Just a couple of months previously, I had seen the same industrialist attend a session where the former CEO had made a brilliant presentation on how he had taken his company to the premier position it enjoyed today.

He answered, 'I don't know the inside story but the news is that he thought he was bigger than the owner and you can't do that and exist in the corporate sector'. *You are getting too big for the boots that I designed for you.*

This thinking was at the core of the whole story of the corporate sector, which he explained to me in just a few words. *You cannot get bigger than the boss in ideas.* It starts from the top, first with the like-minded members on the board. It is put rather neatly, 'he is so easy to get along with'; 'he understands our culture'; or 'he is like-minded'. A polite way of saying, *he toes my line.* And through the organisation, the need to establish like-mindedness takes priority. And company after company chugs along for some years before it is overtaken by the winds of change because change and conformity are not the best of friends.

When you study the psychology of the CEOs who promote this philosophy, there is one common gene in them. These people suffer from insecurity, and lack self-confidence and self-assurance. Any disagreement is seen as a threat to their position and they quell it with all the might of their authority.

It is only the confident and the secure that allow discontent, which is constructive in nature. They do not tie their self-esteem with the aprons of hundred per cent agreements. Their language is different. *Can you give me your perspective? What do you think about it? Tell me more about that idea of yours.*

C.K. Prahalad, the management guru, while addressing corporate chiefs said this: 'To know how effective your Board is, ask how many of them will stand up to you and take differing positions'.

What constructive discontent means is to accept that there is another side of the issue that needs to be seen as much as my side of the issue. Walt Whitman puts it rather neatly when he asks, 'Have you learnt lessons only from those who admired you and are more tender with you and stood aside for you. Have you not learnt from those who brace themselves against you despite the passage with you?'

If we take this advice seriously (and I believe we ought to), the first thing we need to do is to recruit some rebels on the boards of the companies. The best example of constructive discontent can be set at the board level. In the present day, it is common practice that all resolutions presented at the board level are passed unanimously, in almost all companies.

Whose job is it to produce such an environment in an organisation? Clearly, of the leader of the organisation. We would do well to heed another management thinker, who puts it this way: 'It is the job of the leader to create an atmosphere that transforms antagonism into creative energy'.

If constructive discontent is so important for the organisation to lap up new ideas, why does it not happen? The reason is, that it is hard work to fashion a culture that appreciates the creative power of conflict. Maintaining a status quo is a lot less cumbersome and less risky. Discontent, when not harnessed properly, results in chaos and that becomes the worry of the inadequate leader.

When the culture of discontent is established at the board level, people in the organisation will become comfortable with the concept. Only a few Indian companies have shown that kind of courage and handled the change of liberalisation with some degree of success. TISCO is one of those few companies. I have followed the progress of this company from the 1970s and am convinced that it is through the participative and fear-free environment that J.R.D. Tata set up in the company, that it managed to not only emerge a winner but went on to become a global player. Years after he left the corporation, the company culture of TISCO has been established and consolidated, so it has monkeys who dare to climb the ladder and go for the bananas hanging at the top.

Sir Francis Bacon said much the same in another way: 'We rise to great heights through a winding staircase'. And the companies that imbibe this philosophy will survive the change in this century. The rest will perish.

T ODAY, I can sit back and laugh over what were once the most painful three years of my life. Every week on Wednesdays, I would visit both my psychiatrist and clinical psychologist—to deal with my bout of clinical depression. The reference paper that the psychiatrist asked me to carry to his colleague, the psychologist, contained the following diagnosis:

Mr Dinesh Kumar has an acute case of perkitis, caused by the grief of redundancy without adequate mental preparation. His symptoms suggest a withdrawal syndrome of perks suddenly taken away from him, without giving him any notice of the same. Additionally, he may be suffering from carditis; a common corporate mental affliction due to the loss of the company credit card. He has been advised to take:
RX
Prothiaden 75mg (one at bed time)
Tab Anxit 25mg (at bedtime)
Weekly visits advised
Referred for therapy intervention.

When I was finally taken off the therapy and medication, the two doctors called me into their office. The more senior of the two said, 'We are happy with the progress you have made. In fact, you are a success story for us and we will be presenting you as a case study at the next conference of psychiatrists.'

'Three years is a long time, Doctor', I said in a feeble voice. The frequent medication had taken a heavy toll on me.

'That's not very long, when it's common knowledge that perkitis is an almost incurable disease. Most people carry it to their grave.' The junior shrink, who had a long nose and floppy ears, replied gravely.

'Are there any chances of a relapse?' I asked.

'We don't have enough established data about this disease but there are ways to reduce the chances', one of them said.

'Like what?' I inquired.

'Like reliving those traumatic moments, as they happened,' said the senior shrink.

'How was your last day?' questioned the junior doc.

'And what happened after that?' The senior piped in.

'Don't resist any negative thoughts that you may get. The more you resist them, the more they will come, and the more powerful they will become', junior shrink intoned.

'Share your thoughts on these traumatic experiences with friends and family', advised the senior.

'Share your feelings,' said junior.

'Give vent to your thoughts,' from senior.

And finally, 'Don't bottle things up, said the junior shrink.

So, I relived the terribly painful last moments of my life in the corporate world. It flashed through my memory almost like a near-death experience, in split seconds. I share it here with you.

I sobbed uncontrollably on the last day at office, when a mean-looking, four-foot nothing from the internal audit department came to collect the company credit card. He cut it into pieces right in front of me. You should have seen the glee on his face when he handed over the acknowledgement. The cold-hearted way in which he did this made me wonder which category of species internal auditors belong to—certainly not to the same one that you and I do. To hurt a retiring colleague like that was downright cruel. His one mean act created a vacuum around me and the whole world began to look dark and gloomy.

My eyes were wet when I left my room, and I looked longingly back at the chair from which I was cutting the umbilical cord forever. What a source of power it had been! (the chairs were made high for us so that we could glower down at people without appearing to) What will I do without it? I wondered sadly to myself.

Diana, my secretary, could not control her emotions either. She had always been my pillar of emotional support in the company. There was not one thing she was not willing to do to keep me in a happy and invigorated mood. She could even recall 200 telephone numbers without looking at the directory!

It was not the loss of pay I was crying over. It was the loss of the perks! Pay was nothing—it was all there in the salary slip. The perquisites—or the expense account—now that was a different story!

With that little plastic card, I could take out my family of 22, aged from eight to 80, to the swankiest restaurant for a gourmet meal, with wine and all thrown in.

Now, to have to look at the right side of the menu before selecting a dish is too much to bear even in three-star restaurants! Even thinking about it is depressing me already!

I had mastered the art of swirling my scotch in the executive way and selecting the right wine for the right food. Red wine with white meat...or was it the other way around? It was so long ago, it is hard to recall now. How I loved holding a goblet of cognac between my palms, so that the warmth of my hands would produce that special vapoury whiff. I can sometimes still remember that aroma when I am having my rum and water . . .

It was not only while travelling that there was so much fun. Life at home was also one big party. My good friends from other companies would accompany my wife and I to many different restaurants. Of course, we took turns to pick up the tab. There was always enough left-over food to carry home for our two dogs (corporate dogs have the same hierarchy as their owners—the ones for which the vet comes to visit in the owner's Mercedes don't normally mix with those who travel to the vet in a Ford).

Now my good friends have made some new good friends. And the stewards look the other way when I go back to these places for someone else's birthday party.

International travel was another big lark. With the 'companion free' ticket, I could take my wife along and spoil her without spending a dollar of my own.

Our business partners and their wives took care of everything. One did not have to lift a finger to do anything on these trips. Everyone knows how important international cooperation is but in the business world, it is made of six-sigma quality! And allowances for overseas trips were meagre then.

My third wife has a bone to pick with me for not taking her to Russia. You see, she is not ready to travel by 'cattle' class. She is a bit choosy, isn't she? I mean, if I can come down to rum and water, she could also make some sacrifices! Wouldn't you think so?

Then there were those fat packets you received at Board meetings. The notes were always crisp, and you would normally get four packets in one day, so that you could collect the sitting fee, the air travel and the out-of-pocket expense from four companies. The expenses were charged to my company too, so all of it was free moolah. Four fat packets can earn many perks at home, too!

I have just returned home from visiting the doctors. I still have to see them every three months. They are happy the way things are going for me but they have cautioned me that it will be a long haul before I can see signs of a complete recovery.

They have advised me to drive past all the portals of my past power like hotels, and corporate offices, car showrooms and those swanky restaurants. The process of desensitising must continue. I must continue to relive those moments of glory and share my feelings with near and dear ones.

When I took out the purse to pay their fee, the senior doctor said. 'Don't worry about that. You have introduced us to something we can now specialise in— corporate grief. We had not realised such vast opportunities existed in this field. There is enough to go around.' And they waived their fee.

I saw the junior shrink wink at the senior as only shrinks can do.

And I understood what they meant when I saw two gleaming cars in the porch.

Part II

On
Leadership
(Or the Lack of It)

A Crash Course in Quality

10

T HAT JIMMY Nagarwala of Kibuta Steel is a man of few words, highly result-oriented, and who tolerates no nonsense is a well-known fact. Equally well known is that this man, in his early fifties, is at his best in strategy planning on long international flights, when he has finished downing his second after-dinner cognac, or between two holes of a golf course. What readers don't know is that he is also a man who has a short attention span and, therefore, he reads what his secretary carefully marks for him on the newspapers. He only glances through the book reviews to get some sense of what the world of management is all about, and with that limited overview does not hesitate to hold forth on the latest concepts in management.

Being the public face of his company, he makes it a point to regularly attend the conferences at Davos and enrolls himself for all the overseas programmes for the top management.

He has just returned from a crash course in total quality control in Japan. We take a peep into his first meeting with his management committee after his return from Japan.

Gentlemen,

As you all know I have been to Japan to attend a three-day crash course on quality. I can say without hesitation that these were the three most productive days of my entire career. It would not be an overstatement if I were to say that I learnt more in these three days than what I have learnt in the last three years. I used to have a vague idea of how the Japs had licked their quality problem but now I know how exactly they managed it. I want to give you a quick run through on what was taught to us, so that you can go ahead and implement the programme.

His emphasis on the word 'you' is received with grunts all around because Jimmy *sahib* thinks that it is for the functionaries to function while the boss man takes the creamy layer.

Dr Matsuo told us that it was important for the top management to assume the leadership role in initiating and installing TQM in their companies. His view was that quality cannot and must not be delegated, and that in the absence of top leadership assuming direct responsibility, all efforts in TQM would most surely fail.

I totally agree with this concept but I wish I could follow his advice. I have, therefore, decided to promote manager, quality, to the position of vice-president, with immediate effect. Henceforth, he will report directly to me and not to the VP (manufacturing). I know it is a quick promotion for him but we have no time to lose.

Pam, the media relations manager and a favourite of the managing director (MD) for professional and not so professional reasons, flutters her long eyelashes and says, 'exactly'. That she receives a cold response from others is totally lost on Jimmy *sahib*, who continues:

Dr Matsuo also said that the MDs themselves should navigate the ship called quality and not board it as mere passengers. I will be doing this whenever I am in town; for the rest of the time our newly appointed vice-president (quality assurance) will be the man at the deck as the ship's first officer. Please consider the instructions you get from him to have my blessings.

The naval analogy failed to impress the audience because they knew that the boss man was again passing the buck. Only Pam intervened with 'well said'.

Professor Yamada told us that the most common mistake he found that the management made was that they were forever chasing results. Quarterly results, half-yearly results and annual results. He emphasised that the results were a consequence of the processes we install in the companies. He advised us to concentrate on the processes or methods of doing work in sales, marketing, and design and in all other departments. "Take care of the processes and the results will take care of themselves", Professor Yamada advised. The Japanese will consider any result, however perfect, an accident or just plain good luck, unless it is backed by a stable process of high reliability. His words of wisdom still ring in my ears. It is something like our karma stuff.

I have decided to follow just that approach. That is to say, that all of you in your departments from now on will pay more attention to the processes involved rather than chasing results. The vice-president (manufacturing) will give you all the guidance and help you need in this area.

The vice-president (manufacturing) looked up as if to say that in that case he should have been the one to attend the course.

Professor Puntambe told us that the worst enemy of quality was the inter-departmental rivalry that exists in most companies. Each department blamed the other when things went wrong. There were silos of separation between the departments. The only way, he said, to solve this age-old problem was to "treat the next process as your customer". He said that each person or department was a recipient of the efforts of another person or department and, therefore, deserved to be treated with respect and consideration reserved for external customers. To emphasise the importance of the concept, the Professor said, "remember that only happy internal customers can make for happy external customers". This is a wonderful concept and a practical way of putting an end to all the inter-departmental bickering in our company. From now on, the managers of departments will move their offices to the upstream department to fully understand the need of their internal customers. They can also practice the just-in-time concept because they will know on a continual basis as and when more material is required from their department by their internal customer.

The vice-president (marketing and sales) wanted to know where his managers would be located since he had a long list of small and big customers. Jimmy *sahib* knew that he was stumped. He stuttered and stammered and said, 'Till I find an answer to this one, ask your managers to stay put.' Then he continued:

We had the privilege of having practising managers share their experiences with us. And one of them told us that managements often based their decisions on opinions, and that solutions based on opinions were nothing but Band-Aid, quick-fix ones. He advised us to dig for the facts behind all the problems to know the real causes, otherwise we would be attacking only the superficial issues and the problems would soon return. I am personally convinced of this approach to solve quality problems on a permanent basis. My advice, therefore, is to dig for facts and in fact, more facts, until you get to the root cause. They said unless the root causes are identified, we will continue to live from crises to crises, and constantly stay in a fire-fighting mode. I am sure you will not spare any effort in this direction.

Jimmy *sahib* was getting tired but he still had more material to share. He asked for coffee, which was served to him in one of his special collection of mugs which always had some unmentionable inscriptions/ risqué cartoons embossed on them. He doggedly went on:

The Japanese were emphatic about the use of a statistical approach to problem solving. They told us to apply statistical tools like the seven tools of quality control, fish-bone diagrams, control charts, run charts, statistical dispersion, data sheets, and Parreto diagrams. It was recommended that we look for statistical dispersion in our data for that is where the clues to problem solving will be found. Being a person with a commercial background, most of the statistical stuff went over my head.

The vice-president (R&D) whispered to his neighbour, 'Like most other important things'.

Jimmy *sahib* continued:

They spent the better part of the day on the PDCA cycle. That is we plan a process first, then install it, check for results and then act on those results. He said that by continuously improving the processes we could make the PDCA cycle tighter and that helped to keep the processes under continuous scrutiny and improvement. That is how we approach zero defect levels in our work.

As we are short of time, I will send you all a copy each of my notes for your detailed perusal.

Jimmy *sahib*, finally sensing some restlessness in his audience, proceeded towards his concluding remarks:

For the most part, I agree with the Japanese and their approach to quality, but I do not think I can agree with their time frames. Professor Yamada was of the view that it took five to six years for the TQM efforts to take strong and permanent roots in a company. It was only later that the constitution and the character of the company changed. He explained it further by saying that in a large company the process of training and education itself took three to four years and the idea was to spread awareness in the ordinary people of the company. The Japanese, as you know are very slow and deliberate people in whatever they do. I told them I have a time span of one year in mind. I am sure you will not let me down in our combined effort in the achievement of our common goal. Best of luck, gentlemen.

A smart Alec, sitting at the far end of the table, out of hearing range of the MD muttered, 'Amen' and the meeting ended.

Postscript:

- The company failed miserably in its effort to introduce TQM because it ignored the important advice given by the Japanese.
- The top manager abdicated his direct responsibility. It was too great a change to be caused without his total support.
- The company was trying to move from an authoritarian command and control structure to a decentralized *next process being the king* concept. This paradigm shift is just not possible until there is a paradigm shift by the top manager's personal philosophy.
- Education and training of the rank and file in a company takes years to achieve.
- A lot of time and money was spent without any results, causing frustration and lack of credibility within the company.
- Adopting TQM means adopting a new philosophy of management.

These things were of little concern to Jimmy *sahib*. He had discovered another toy called SAP which he was planning to install, not realising that for a software like SAP to succeed, the systems in the company had to be totally transparent. Transparency and Jimmy *sahib* were at opposite ends of the pole.

Swing Your Fortune on the Golf Course

11

Strictly for those who work for golfing CEOs

I F ONE were to collect the statistics on this interesting nugget, I'm positive that they would prove that the combined fortune of corporate golfers around the world, on any Sunday morning, would be more than the total wealth of all the nations put together!

A major global aviation company was considering a friend of mine to represent them in India. They almost came to a decision on the issue, when he was asked this very vital question: Do you play golf?

My friend needed advice on how to answer this tricky question. I am going to counsel him on how to lie without *actually* lying. That is how high the stakes are for him! And that is how important this international corporate game is. One would indeed be a slow learner if one treated a golf course as an ordinary parcel of acreage and dismissed its importance.

In a 'golfing company', you can ignore the game only at the peril of your corporate career. However, before you rush off to send an email to your NRI brother/sister to send you a golf set, finish reading this . . .

If you are a middle manager, start playing golf in a distantly located golf course, where the chance of seeing your boss is next to nil. Hone your game quietly, keeping it top secret, because you do not belong on a golf course yet! You are supposed to be at the workplace, morning, noon and night, working your butt off. So that when you do emerge on the fairway, you'll hear them say, 'That chap Nimmy has a natural swing!' You don't want to appear to be a self-conscious player. There are going to be enough pressures on you as it is (working and playing). So you must wait for the right time.

What is the right time? When you are asked by your boss, 'Have you ever considered playing golf?' Be prudent and say, 'I always thought that it would be at the cost of my work . . .'

Your boss will probably reply, 'It doesn't have to be that way. I play golf but I don't let it interfere in my work. It is all about balance, my boy.'

Just sigh in response.

Treat the invitation with caution. You have *not* arrived in the golfing fraternity until you have *really* arrived. That takes diplomacy and calls for many extraordinary managing-the-boss skills, like sucking up to the boss.

Pick up a few golfing joke books but for God's sake don't try to be too smart and start telling them between the holes. It would be smarter to send them to your bosses by email, so that they can repeat them as their own jokes (remember to laugh as if you were hearing them for the first time though!).

Learn to say 'great shot' and 'bad luck'; 'looks like it's not your day', at the appropriate places. But never, *ever* give him advice him on his follow through! Remember that it is *only* the boss's boss's privilege to correct his game. So maintain a strict corporate hierarchy—the golden rule being, when in doubt, keep shut!

Learn to slice intentionally into the rough, in order to neutralise your stroke advantage (should you have been stupid enough to gain it in the first place). Occasionally, pretend that you have lost the ball in the bushes. Give your boss enough space, even when through his sheer stupidity, he muffs up on the last few holes (he will call it an off day—nod your head vigorously to that feeble excuse). Let him remain a stroke or two ahead of you. The trick is to give him enough of a challenge and yet be careful not to overdo it.

However honest the boss may be at the workplace (although I have not met many honest golfing CEOs), don't be shocked if he cheats copiously on the golf course. He will do it in many different ways, like moving the ball to get a better lie for the next stroke. He will pretend to lose count of the number of strokes between holes. If he asks you for the score, state one stroke less than the actual figure.

Also be the first to take out your wallet to pay the caddies. Your boss will never have the right change, or even the inclination to pay the caddies, anyway.

At the nineteenth hole, when he is freshening up, order his preferred drinks. If the boss says, 'I thought I would have a glass of beer before switching over to gin and tonic.' Tell him not to worry because you were thinking of having a gin and tonic anyway! That's what it means to be a yes-man!

Now that you have played golf with the boss for about a year, it is time for you call him home. Hold your tongue until he says, 'When are we coming home for a meal?' (don't look baffled, he is not referring to his wife as well, but using the royal *we* here). Ring up his secretary and ask him to check when the boss and his wife would be free to come home for dinner. You could ask him yourself but that way, only the boss and you will know about it. If you talk to his secretary, half the company will know about it. Can you think of an easier way of building brand equity?

To find out the boss' preferred diet (and his wife's as well), turn to the private network for this privileged information. He will then gush with surprise, 'How did you know that I prefer single malts to scotch' and 'Ever since Blue Label has been available, I haven't touched Black Label!' Never put yourself in the position of having to say, 'I'm so sorry, I don't have dry sherry', if that is what the good lady wants (unless of course you want to throw away the Blue Label advantage).

By now you will be accompanying your corporate buddies to Ooty, Kodaikanal and Eagleton for golfing trips. And you can now tell the odd golfing joke for every three or four that they come up with. Always start your joke with 'Your joke reminds me of . . .' Remember to let him keep the initiative. If he likes raunchy jokes (my experience tells me that the dirtier the joke, the more they like it), open with, 'I don't know whether I should be telling you this one . . .' and then go ahead and repeat it with lots of sly winks and grins.

At this stage, you can expect to start receiving golf balls and occasionally, a club to replace your worn-out ones. Next you will get the boss's scarcely-used set, as he now has acquired a better one.

This is the time to start boning up on all the famous golf courses of the world, like St Andrews, Turnburry, Pebble Beach and Glen Abbey (in the happy event you are invited to go on golfing holidays with the boss).

You will also notice some changes at the workplace, in the form of higher (though totally undeserved) bonuses, an out-of-turn promotion and a move into the wood-panelled office in the main corporate building, and a secretary and chauffeur of your own. Don't worry if your job description has not changed too much. Worry about your designation instead. You are now at a policy-making level. You deserved to get there after all that hard work!

Persist until you get a whole new set of clubs. Now you have truly arrived! The gates of St Andrew's and all the other top-notch golf courses will open for you. You will get to play golf in the Champagne district of France—and sip champagne at the nineteenth hole!

The final obstacle to the golf course is indeed an arduous one. You have to negotiate it with extreme care, as it is a 'do or die' situation. A lot is at stake. One false move, like jumping the sequence given above, is fraught with danger. Do it will well and success will be yours!

I once worked for a golfing CEO but got stuck at Step 1. The golfing coach gave me up as a bad joke and advised me to stick to a physical sport like jogging. 'Golf', he said, 'requires a much higher mental calibre and concentration', far beyond the level that I seemed to possess.

I not only survived but also did fairly well in the company. How, you may wonder.

I did the next best thing. I married the CEO's daughter!

By the Law of
Averages 12

EVERY JOB has some hazards attached to it. There are, as we know, no free lunches. My kind of work has its own share of perils attached. One of these is that my first point of contact is the CEO. I wish I had a choice in the matter. I have got to get their approval to be listed in the company. Unless they nod their heads, it is a no-go situation, not only for me but also for those who belong to my breed and practise my creed.

The result of being frequently seen with the CEO is that the speed with which the finance man clears your bill is directly proportional to the ease and frequency of access you have with the CEO. Finance managers are so good at losing consulting bills that they need to be impressed and kept in good humour.

They are good for starting various initiatives as long as the donkey's work is done by others. They are likely to say, 'Why don't you write a few introductory remarks for me so that you can glide in your presentation after my remarks and there is a seamless transition.' *Seamless* is meant to impress me. The idea, of course, is to help me.

As they sit for the first few minutes of the three-day workshop, they like hearing things like: *you are fortunate to be working for a company* (meaning the CEO), *which has taken this path-breaking initiative to launch this programme. I was talking to your CEO on the way to this hall and he fully shared with me the concern that training and development of the people is of paramount importance in your company. He also told me that he considers human capital development an investment for the future.*

By the way, this opening does bring some broad smiles on the faces of the CEOs and oils my way to a more enduring presence in the company.

I was talking about the hazard of having to meet them. One other common hazard comes out like this: 'Mr Kumar, you travel a great deal. I am looking for a brilliant guy to look after our project division. The incumbent is a pretty average guy and I have had had enough of him.'

I can't help observing the irony of the situation. Here is an average guy asking another pretty average guy to find a brilliant guy. Since CEOs generally don't like hearing 'No' for an answer, I have to be circumspect about it.

If the measure of a CEO's sharpness is the size of his spacious office, loaded with the curios from the world, with large windows overlooking a lush green lawn, and if it includes an exclusive secretary, a private shower and a loo (or, in some cases, even a private pantry), then of course the breed must very sharp. But I am not sure these should be the measures. I am not even sure that I have met many brilliant CEOs. The most I have come across are pretty average like me, unless I have been keeping the wrong company.

Coming back to their incessant demand for high fliers, I find that it is not only a tall order but also an impossible one to execute. We all know that this overpopulated world houses not more than 5 per cent who are high fliers, and about the same percentage low fliers. The bulk belongs to my category, high average in some areas, low average in some others, but on the average, pretty average. They are the bread and butter of the company. They are the ones that provide balance and stability. They are the ones who can work in a plateau, not seeking constant highs to stay invigorated and excited.

And the funny part is that the CEO would have, just the previous day, laboured over in a leadership seminar, saying something like this: 'One of the roles of great leaders is to get extraordinary results out of ordinary people. That is what leadership is all about. Getting the best out of the various skills placed at your disposal. People who come to us are human raw material and it is our responsibility to shape their futures by providing them skills through continuation training.'

I was very fond of an American CEO until I read his autobiography and read about the retirement deal that he had put together for himself. He says many silly things in his book but the silliest of all is that he would get rid of 10 per cent of his lowest performers every year and replace them with brilliant outsiders. I have always wondered whether he was not churning out the average of the world, training them, and getting rid of his trained people who, with his company's badge, were finding better jobs for themselves.

One day I will have to tell my dear CEOs that as a counsellor I see a lot of professionals who are going through some trauma or the other. Fair enough. We all go through traumas, ups and downs, lows and highs. It is a very human thing to happen but the ones who find this difficult to accept and cope with, are these high fliers, these brilliant guys the CEOs are constantly hunting. One trigger of failure, one rejection of some kind, and one failure in a job interview sends them into depression.

It is the average, well-rounded, work-within-my limitation people who seem to cope well in their lives. If only I could show them evidence and statistics to prove that the most brilliant fade away at the middle managements level and often work for people less brilliant than they are. Occasionally, I manage to get the material they want but in most such cases you start hearing that 'the guy you got me is too much of an individualistic to be a team person. He thinks no end of himself. It is his way or the highway. He seems to rub everyone the wrong way.'

Arey, you are the one who wanted an exceptional person and now that you have one, what are you complaining about? And wasn't it you who was telling me the other day that you welcome constructive discontent because it is only then that the best in the company comes out?

But they still insist and I still continue trying, for the brilliant ones, and since brilliant people are always on job rotation, I have no difficulty finding them replacements.

I am writing this sitting on a stone barstool with my feet dipped in the swimming pool, with a gin and tonic by my side, and my grandchildren swimming in the pool. Not bad going for an average chap!

Who wants to burn the proverbial midnight oil?

My advice? Be average. Hire average. Train them. Keep them.

Viagra for the Drooping Market 13

ENTREPRENEURS AROUND the world are probably kicking themselves (hard!) for not having thought of this amazingly innovative idea to corporatise the oldest profession on the planet.

John Timble of Australia has done just that, by launching a company called Daily Planet, the first public limited company in the world that offers 'products' and 'services' that lie in the scope of the business just mentioned.

John's initiative has received rave reviews around the world. Indian business newspapers have also written laudatory editorials dedicated to John's unique venture. The papers have even suggested that an Initial Public Offering (IPO) by the company would be 'just be the sort of thing to perk the *sagging* business up'.

His idea was even called the 'Viagra of sorts for the *drooping* market' (italics mine) by one particularly witty newspaper. Such a positive response from the business press is bound to receive even more favourable attention from the international investing community.

Being a management consultant for over 40 years, I sent in a consultancy proposal to John, to offer my assistance to maximise the Return on Investment (ROI) on his newfound business. For obvious reasons of confidentiality, I can give only a broad overview of my proposals. Given below are some of the suggestions I made:

Happy Hour Discount

Akin to the discounts that many bars offer, a 50 per cent discount would be offered to clients on their way home from work. Considering the de-stressing factor as proven by medical studies, physical activity is highly recommended on the way home.

Maximum utilisation of capacity is an important factor in business competitiveness, as is the inventory turnover. Recent studies of the Indian industry show, that it is the improvement in these two areas that has made the industry more efficient than in the past.

You will observe that the concept of marginal costing, after the break-even point has been reached, is applied here. The intention is to recover the fixed costs and the cost of consumables like electricity and water, after the break-even has been achieved.

Frequent User Bonus

Similar to the loyalty programmes currently offered by airlines, points would be given on an accrual basis. The more 'interesting' choices that are selected would mean more points accrued for the user.

Earning customer loyalty in any business is a much-desired aim. It must be the endeavour of all businesses to create a bank of loyal customers. They are our best referrals and the marketing costs, with loyal customers, are almost zero.

Inclement Weather Discount

The company could think of an inclement weather discount, for those who brave through snow, heat, blizzard or deluge, to keep the top line intact in adverse business conditions.

Sales of many items of business reduce during some climatic conditions. For example, the sale of generators during the rainy season, when the mains supply is good. Instead of laying off your people and cutting down production, sell to those who have the holding capacity at a lower price.

Senior Citizen Discount

Those above 65 years could be offered a 50 per cent discount, on the premise that, barring a few exceptions, the transaction time for such customers will be low and therefore the real return on investment will be high.

Here the attempt is to create a win-win situation for the customer and the establishment. The benefit of a lower cost of transaction is shared between the business and the customer.

Loyalty Discount

The cost of marketing is negligible for loyal and repeat customers.

I have been loyal to Standard Chartered bank for my credit card, although I am under great pressure from all the major card companies, including the topnotch banks offering alternatives. It would be a good strategy for the bank to recognise my unstinting loyalty.

Strategic Alliances with Other Service Industries

I have strongly recommended a strategic tie-up with other service industries like airlines and hotels. Airlines could drop their weary customers to the nearest branch of the business on the way to the guest's hotel. It would be a sort of room service in reverse. Similarly, the hotel industry could add this additional service in their current array of room services offered.

This is about creating a synergy between similar businesses. Air Lanka is a fine example of it. You buy their ticket and forget about the rest. The airport transfers and hotel accommodation are part of the package. Now, here is an opportunity for the airline to add even more value to its existing package.

Group Discount

Just as any other industry offers discounts for bulk purchases, this concept should also be tried in this sunshine industry.

Let me ask you a question. When you make bulk purchases, don't you expect additional discounts?

All-inclusive Packages

I have also proposed that all-inclusive packages should be considered by the management. For example, early-birds, inclement weather, and senior citizens could be clubbed together in a scheme called, *the more-you-do-the-more-you-get.*

A word of advice for wise marketers. Do not compartmentalise businesses. If a project requires all its

requirements from one industrial house, doesn't it deserve
special treatment? What would it be like if customers
bought generators from you and motors from the
competition, when you are also in the motor business?

Corporate Links

It would be necessary to offer corporate memberships. This would help provide the base load
necessary for any kind of business.

It would be a foolish business house that does not
realise the financial muscle power of the corporations,
and hence, this suggestion has been made.

The Cheery Cherry Pop Top Discount

For the momentous, first-time user.

It should be the endeavour of all businesses to latch
on to start-up projects. Once the start-up project has
standardised its products and services, it will experience
an advantage in all future expansions.

The Divorce Special

To help get over those difficult days.

When your customer's business is going through a bad
phase, stick with him through the adversity he faces. He
will remember your support when he recovers.

Early-bird Discounts

This is something like the super-saver apex fares
that the airlines offer.

Booking your production capacity in advance is a
clever idea. However, don't go overboard. Earmark only
a small portion to provide psychological security. The
advance given on this account can be forfeited in the
event of cancellation.

Needless to add, my services include advice on acquisitions and mergers on a global basis, to exploit the economy of scales of this nascent business. In fact, being a specialist on this type of joint venture, I am sure that a suitable arrangement could be made to franchise this business in India.

I have no doubt that a man as clever as John, will not miss the merit of my proposal, and will soon send me a ticket to Melbourne, where the company headquarters are located. As a sweetener, I have accepted to receive my fee in kind, appreciating that cash flows will be required for the consolidation of business in the first few years.

I have also no doubt that my discerning readers will have observed that I have provided insights to their businesses by sharing my expertise. Invitations to cocktails and dinner will be welcome in a five-star setting.

Finally, a Marwari vice-president of a large business group in India taught me a corporate mantra, which I still remember. I have used his advice to great advantage in my business life. He said, 'Inventory in your warehouse is like constipation in the body. Be sure, it will cause you sickness. As all healthy people keep their stomach clear, you must keep your inventory turnover high and the warehouse empty.'

Being 75 in the Boardroom 14

I T MUST be the number 75. The age, I mean, of the directors. Not the *exit* age but the *entry* age. This is the age when you cross over from ignorance to wisdom, from immaturity to maturity, from time to timelessness and from a whole bottle of scotch to just one whole peg.

Therefore, I am not sure what the raging debate is about. Some directors say that they must go at 75 because they are past their prime. They say, when things are happening at the speed of thought, these people must make place for the young. The future belongs to the young. To the Bushes and the Blairs of the world and not to the Atal*ji*s, and their ilk.

Others say that if we do a silly thing like that, we will lose the good old veterans of the Indian industry. Not fair, they say, when there is no retirement age for politicians, why should there be a retirement age for corporate leaders? *Double standards*, they shout.

The government says that many other countries have similar rules. Their opponents remark that if you quote other countries, then let us talk about a maximum of two terms for Indian politicians, like they have in the US for their presidents.

Ask any senior executive who is privileged to sit on the Board of a company and chances are that 99.9 out of a 100 that he will back me on the age issue because he is comfortable with the Board. He has experience with them. He has worked with them. He can predict their behaviour.

You see, when you have escorted these senior directors from their cars through the corridors of power to the Boardroom and said, 'Mind your step, there is one more step to climb, a bit steep. Ah, there we are'. And when you have positioned them next to their chair, where they can feel their way and sit down. And when you have taken their cane to be kept in a corner of the Boardroom and they have thanked you, chances are that he will not ask many questions of you. The Board member knows that he will need your help when he is performing the journey in reverse.

Why am I being such a hypocrite when I am talking about my experience in the third person? Why not shoot straight from the hip?

I have been simultaneously an executive and a director and, therefore, have seen both sides of the coin.

As an executive, I was in charge of escorting the directors, keeping their magnifying glasses at the right places, and seating them and the other executives in such a manner that there was someone ready to help the old fogies find the right page and the right resolution, otherwise they would have been lost in the maze of paper work. If the company was a government company, the job was an onerous one because for every resolution there was a thick appendix titled *Appendix A- Explanatory Notes to Resolution 1*. Frankly, these were no more than cover-our-asses notes.

You have directors who go gaga over the performance of the companies when they read that the company has made 33.3 crore profit when it is actually 3.33 crore. It is just that they can't read that little decimal point.

Post-Board meeting life is also so easy. The lunch after the board meeting at the swankiest hotel is a brief affair because most of them need a nanny to put a bib around their neck to ensure they don't soil their wrinkled suits. They need just one small gin and tonic to transport them into bliss. Now tell me which of the executives will not back me for the entry age of directors being 75 and not a day less.

And it is around this age that former finance joint secretaries begin to cash on their past favours and earn representations on the Boards of companies on behalf of banks or financial institutions . . . . So, you see, it is a popular pastime. No longer playing bridge, they want to play the Board!

Market Segmentation 15

D URING ONE of my travels, I happened to be seated next to a big, burly, bursting-at the-seams hotelier. If he were a true representative of the hospitality industry, to which he said he belonged, he broke one of the long-held myths—that we consultants are the most verbose species that ever inhabited planet Earth. I know my breed has a propensity for verbosity, but this gentleman was in a totally different league.

We may talk much but at least we keep the volume and pitch low, measured, and are circumspect as we look for simultaneous feedback on every word of utterance.

You know what? I got exactly 133 words through in the 130 minutes flight from Bangalore to Delhi. That was about a word a minute, including articles like *a/an/and/the*. And that too when he was swallowing something. He had this fascinating ability to munch and talk simultaneously.

He asked me what my specialty was and I said, 'Market segmentation'. Those two words excited him no end and he said, 'Boss, you must help our industry'. 'Sure', I replied, rubbing my hands in glee, as I smelt a brand new opportunity.

It was my turn to speak and so, I told him in a serious consultant-like manner, that no problem defies a solution if it is properly identified and is accurately described. It is in the clear enunciation of the problem itself that we look for clues for possible solutions.

He said, 'Boss whatever we do, we never seem to please one segment of our clientele and those are the big chiefs of the Indian corporations.'

'That is sad', I said.

'Yes, it is. In our industry we know that it is the high-value customers like CEOs who make or break the industry but we can't seem to please them enough.'

'Whatever you do?' I asked.

'Yes. You should see the feedback forms they scribble on and leave behind. *This is not good. That was horrible. The airport pick-up was ordinary. There was a long delay at the reception. There are no specialty items in the room fridges.* It's just one complaint after the other.'

When we landed at Palam airport we exchanged business cards and I promised to keep in touch. And as if the north Indian breeze had something to do with it, he said, *'Kharche ka fiqr mat karna. Problem solve honi chahiye.* In any case, the expenses will be shared by the industry.'

We consultants like these open-ended, carte blanche assignments. In simple words it means, *expenses at actuals.* There was another attraction in this assignment. I could combine it with others. This was a case of 'a creamy layer', if that is the right phrase to describe the situation.

Wherever I broached the subject of quality of service in the hospitality industry, the CEOs exploded with anger.

'It's not quality, it's plain and simple trash at seven-star prices,' said one of them. And to explain his agitation he said, 'How dare they send a mid-segment car for an airport pick-up when Mercs are available on call right here in India. I tell you, Dinesh, that this industry has not moved with the times. It is stuck in the 1970s and the 1980s.'

'You mean the standard of cars for the airport pick-up needs to be upgraded to luxury cars', I said, prompting the conversation.

'What has luxury got to do with it? It is a pure and simple case of market segmentation. That is all. The hotels seem to believe in one omnibus segment. And the same old stereotype style of a chauffeur with a couple of newspapers and magazines kept for you to read.'

'You mean, they could improve in the area of on-arrival services?' I asked hesitatingly.

'Exactly, I mean what is the problem of assigning a dedicated and trained hostess from the point of arrival to the point of departure, instead of having to deal with so many different people? A kind of one point of comfort and responsibility.'

'That, you believe, is the majority view?' I asked.

'Ask anyone from my community and he will tell you how exasperated we feel.'

I decided to do exactly that.

At my next port of call, I brought up the subject with another of the *community*. This one was sure of the need for change but he put it across in a rather sophisticated manner.

'For sure, we have a wish list that the hospitality industry needs to address,' he said softly. 'There is, I believe, a strong case for having a separate gym, sauna and massage parlour for CEOs, where the environment is more genteel and conducive to relaxation, and not the kind of muscle-building, smelly and sweaty set-up that the hotels currently have.'

'Exactly,' I said emphatically.

'And they could also think in terms of a putting a green at the site or nearby, where we can do some putting practice before we leave for work. You know what I mean.'

'Yes, I do,' I responded in an equally soft tone.

Then, with a 'cheerio', he left for his next flight.

And so it went on with the problem identification exercise (with another boss).

'Look, I believe that the hospitality industry needs to wake up to the new realities', he said, thumping the table to make his point.

'Which means?, I glided in.

'Which means nothing more than a call to the secretary and asking her what each person's requirements are. Don't we establish customers' needs in our industry? We even write down mandatory and desirable specifications of the products and services before we would even take the first step in designing. Look, I would be a fool to plunge into a new development without being clear on the qualitative requirements. You yourself have been harping on identification of needs.'

I was not sure whether my harps were getting home in most cases.

'That sounds more like a commonsense approach to managing effectively, if a telephone call is all it takes', I said, agreeing with the boss man.

'And saves them the bother of asking, "Is there anything you require, sir?" These are some of the unique selling propositions you need to build in your offerings. We are not asking for the moon, are we?' he said speaking on behalf of the clan.

'While we are at it, is there any other area where you would like to see some sharp improvements in value addition?' I asked

'All I am asking the industry is to stay ahead of time. When the airlines introduced slumberettes, that was the time for the hotel industry to ask itself, what are they doing to upgrade their services?'

'This, of course, will reach the right people, but this may be the time to add to your wish list', I repeated.

'If they can do this much first, we can talk of the second phase. There is a lot more that can certainly be done.'

I knew that I had enough *masala* to build a strong case for a new orientation on the part of the hospitality industry. And all I had to do was to recycle some special consultant phrases, place them in a leather-bound folder and send it to my in-flight friend.

I did exactly that, with no response to all my reminders, till one fine day when I received a letter from his secretary that my recommendations had been forwarded to the industry association and that I would hear from them in the due course.

That due course has yet to happen.

I knew that I had been had.

My wife said philosophically, you win some, you lose some.

The creamy layer had just turned sour.

It is Dangerous to be Good   16

TO BE labelled the meanest CEO in the city is difficult and requires a dedication of a different kind. You would have to invest a lot of time and energy to receiving this title. But if that is your decision, here are some pointers in that regard:

Divide and Rule Policy: I mention this first because it should come easy to Indians—we are all genetically wired that way! First came the Mughals, who taught it to us, then the British gave it a good polish. Now, it is the current breed of politicians who have kept this fine art alive. Therefore, the fine art of dividing and ruling is almost inborn, though dormant, and just waiting to explode.

When Leo comes into the office, you might say, 'Do you know what your friend Scorpio was telling me about you? I couldn't believe my ears that Scorpio, your inseparable colleague, arguably your best conscious keeper, could be saying the things that he was saying.' Shock him with the suddenness of your revelation. Then empathise and say; 'I know how you must feel.' Do the same thing when Scorpio comes into your office. Confuse the living daylights out of them and continue until each one has started sneaking on and about the other.

Then do the same with Virgo, Gemini, and all the others, until no one trusts anyone and you trust no one. That is the divide and rule policy of six sigma quality. Make them paranoid about their colleagues—the second quality we are going to discuss below.

The How and Why of Paranoia: First, it is important to know the pure meaning of paranoia. It means 'long-term dispositions, in a variety of settings, to interpret the actions of others as purposely threatening or demeaning.' It also means the 'attribution of veiled meanings to harmless statements and situations'.

In the early stages, it shows up in 'constantly looking over your shoulders', to the ultimate form: 'are they really my real parents?' While you can certainly leave the domestic side out of it, let me tell you that you would have to be proactively paranoid. This is an essential part of any strategy and it applies equally well here. Remember Nixon? Well he could be your role model but remember that in your case it should fall short of impeachment by the Board of Directors.

In a state of paranoia, imagination plays a great part and being a CEO, imagining the worst-case scenario must come easy to you.

Imagine the worst from your best friends. Shoot if anyone emerges out of the shadows. Then ask questions. Take care of leaving your secretary out of the paranoiac radarscope. You don't know when you might need her, during and, equally importantly, after, working hours. Besides, doesn't she know a bit too much about you? You don't want such a close confidante to turn into a whistle blower!

Besides, your secretary is also your eyes and ears in the organisation. In TQM, we call it the PDCA cycle—you Plan paranoia, you Do the paranoiac schemes, you Check whether they are working for you, and finally, you Act on the feedback. You need her for the feedback phase of the PDCA cycle.

Change Camps: You will best understand this with an example of golf, a game you play so passionately. Play with one set of your senior colleagues for six months and when they begin to confide in you, switch over to the other camp. This policy is complimentary to the first two strategies. This single act will in turn ensure that in your entire organisation no one trusts another.

Never Develop Second-in-commands: Pardon the military terminology. They are needed in the army because you do not know when you will get a bullet biting your brain. There has be a second-in-command to lead the troops if the leader falls. Here you have no intention of falling or leaving. It is fairly easy to achieve this objective.

As soon as your deputy feels secure in his position, spring a surprise on him. Call your finance manager and withdraw his financial powers (well, to be magnanimous, you could limit them to say, Rs 100). What grand plans can he now undertake without the necessary budgetary support? Now you have a toothless tiger raging in a cage. He will leave in frustration sooner than you think.

A classic case study in meanness was reported in *Coward Business Review*. Apparently, a CEO had taken out his deputy for a leisurely lunch to his club. He then introduced a total stranger to the deputy during the meal. While the boss sipped his gin and tonic, he encouraged his deputy to brief the guest about the company and his own functions and responsibilities. After the lunch was over, and the deputy was preparing to leave for a quiet weekend, the CEO said, 'By the way, that guy will be taking over from you on Monday.'

You can use this strategy effectively in your company (the way your face just lit up, it looks like that you liked this idea very much).

Impulsiveness: Impulsiveness is a necessary ingredient for a grand and visionary policy. Just don't let them predict your next move. We use 'unpredictability' in warfare to beat the enemy. Sometimes, we advance, then get into our bunkers to give the enemy an impression that we are recouping and regrouping. They attack and then we counter-attack with a ferocity that is unexpected by the enemy.

You might use impulsiveness in many other ways. One of these that comes to mind, is that when you are having a quiet meal with your colleagues in a nice restaurant, start shouting at the person sitting right in front of you. It is not important who that person is. Yelling without notice is important. It must take everyone by total surprise. With some practice, you will intuitively know when to be impulsive. Another very effective strategy to advance your meanness quotient.

Throw Your Weight Around: You certainly can, even literally speaking! One of the curses of the corporate world is that it does not leave much time to do some serious exercise. A mild game of golf is all one can manage, to stay in breathing condition.

Convert this weakness into your strength. Throw your mighty weight around the shops and offices, and let out a few high-decibel roars at people who are following their boss's policy. Do it in the typical Indian *do-you-know-who-I-am* style. They will get the message and will never mess around with you. A few such visits will also neutralise those few who still count in the organisation.

How many capsules of training you would need, you ask? Well, this chapter is just a trailer of the full movie!

Mr Inverted Snobbery   17

I HAVE recently been very impressed with the young author of *Sack the CEO,* Jeetendra Jain, which is selling like the proverbial hot cake. He has carried out exhaustive research on many role-model CEOs and captured their colourful person-alities, including;

- Mr Crony Capone, suffering from diabetes, who runs his corporation through his favourite cronies.
- Mr Parish Priest, who preaches till you drop dead or become a heart patient.
- Mr Talk the Talk, who suffers from corporate schizophrenia, and only talks but never walks what he talks.
- Mr Volte-face, who suffers from Alzheimer's, and decides to shift his corporate office from Mumbai

Central to the suburbs because his company will save a tidy sum annually. Then changes his mind when the last but one file is about to be moved out to the new location. Why? His wife reminds him that his children will have to travel for three hours every day because the schools in the suburbs are not up to the mark.

- Mr Side Biz, who suffers from osteoporosis, and sets up private companies to route his business to his main company—a chronic Mr 10 per cent.
- Mr Siphon De Cash, a cancer patient, whose main aim in life is to siphon cash for personal use, regardless of the means deployed.

The author has also discussed in detail Mr Last Emperor, a case of HIV, who is stuck to his *gaddi* till he goes to his grave and quashes every rebellion in the bud;

Mr Next Job, that mover and shaker, who always uses his current position to launch a newer and better career (a classic case of Hypermetropia); and

Mr Family Man, suffering from rheumatoid arthritis, under whose tutelage only the family flourishes. The degree of flourish is directly proportional to the degree of closeness of the relationship with Mr Family Man, and Mr Tremble Knees, a hypochondriac, who never signs a single paper, and with the first whiff of trouble passes the buck on to someone else.

But the author has omitted ME, as if I am nothing, as if I am no role model and as if, my off-the-balance sheet costs, and my contribution to the low morale are any less than all the other worthies mentioned above. As if my contribution to corporation sickness is not worth his while!

At the end of the day, authors have to be fair. They cannot choose their favourites and leave out some whose contribution to the corporate world is equally noteworthy, if not more. The only choice I have before me is to tell my story, in my own words:

By the way, I am Mr Inverted Snobbery. In medical terms, I am described as a megalomaniac. And I live by my name with such intensity that my admirers keep saying *wah, wah, kamaal hai.* The space limitation compels me to give you a broad overview of my contribution, through just a few examples.

For example, in a party when the choicest drinks are floating around, I always ask for my rum and coke, even if it takes an hour to get it. In the meantime, I tell others patronisingly, 'Please do carry on gentlemen, I would rather wait for my rum'. I try to do it like the British and sometimes I even succeed. As if they will start before my drink comes and as if I am going to tell them that I have just tucked in two large Black Labels before coming down from my room.

When the entitlement is a big car with a chauffeur thrown in, for instance, I will always switch on the Inverted Snobbery button and say, 'Why do we need a big car for one person's use. We don't need drivers hanging around!'

I really don't care for people who have sweated for over 20 years for just that sort of recognition in front of their family and friends. It is ridiculous to think that they tie their self-esteem to the size of the car.

Or, insisting that I will take a yellow and black cab from the airport to the hotel. *Please don't waste the company's money to send me a hired limo from Mumbai Central. It is such a waste of the company's resources.*

Or, for example, choosing a salad bar for the last dinner in Delhi when the zonal manager and his team were looking forward to a little spoiling at the end of the three-day gruelling schedule.

By the way, setting a tough pace is a part of my personality. I may be bone weary but catch me letting them get away with anything less than a scorching schedule.

Or why do I have to travel by business class within the country? I mean no flight is more than just a couple of hours. I get a devilish delight in seeing a junior executive checking into business class and making him miserable by shouting a loud hello, just in case he has not seen me, or is avoiding eye contact with me.

It is none of my business if people are getting fed up when well-earned perks are kept in abeyance because they are so common and so mundane in their attitude.

I strongly believe that it is enough to grunt in response to someone wishing you good morning. A broad smile is okay for flight attendants but does it behove a corporate chief? No way. A perpetual frown and a constipated look suit my persona.

Eating in the canteen with the juniors when there is a special room for the corporate heavyweights. That helps me to keep my hand on the pulse (but why are these guys eating at such supersonic speed and leaving?)

Some of my colleagues have tried to copy my style but have failed miserably because they have taken exactly the opposite approach.

All they want is a change of décor in the office every year, a change of sofas, new paintings, attached conference rooms, two secretaries (one exclusively to manage the social calendar). Instead, they are stuck with run-of-the-mill snobbery.

My index of Inverted Snobbery kept building up with each promotion. After all, you have to keep learning while you are growing older.

Like I did, by installing a tea kettle in my room to make my own coffee, and for guests too. After all, it is so informal when you make your own coffee and serve it to your guests. I also got rid of the office boy who just carried papers from my office to the secretary and served me coffee. The others had to follow suit. A good example is a good example. Some would say penny-wise pound foolish. My dictum, is take care of pennies and the pounds will take care of themselves.

'Hello, Jatin, how are you? Oh, you want to include me in the revised edition of your book. No, I have not given my copyright to anyone.'

'When, next week? Okay, why don't you meet me in the Woodland lobby at 10 a.m. on Monday. We can talk things over a plate of *dosai*.'

I will be damned if I will pay Rs 200 for a pot of tea at these fancy hotels. Taxes and tips extra.

When I rushed across the lawn from my office to my home to break the good news, the wife was as usual gossiping about me to some stranger and saying, 'He has been in denial. Neither does he know how to enjoy himself nor does he let others. Spoilsport, really.'

Knowing that it will be a gossip of marathon length, and that she will cover the distance, I return to the sanctuary of my office.

What is the Size of Your Office? 18

WHAT ELSE? Why are you corporate fellows so fixated on the size of your anatomical parts? Is your self-esteem so badly tied up in the shape and the size of your body and its part thereof? At least, we (consultants) are a more sober lot. You will never know what is going on in our minds. We keep a serene and wise exterior. We can be smiling even while we are cursing you under our breath. That is the cultural difference between you and us.

Yes, size matters, not only of your office but also of your car, your cell phone, the colour of your credit card, your secretary and many other material things. Let us take each attribute and its size in the reverse order, to see what they mean to you.

What is the size of your secretary? First, do you have one? Is she pretty, perky and petite, who can do five things simultaneously? (Like smiling at the passers-by, doing her nails, keeping one call on hold while talking on another, as she simultaneously glances at the timetable for your next flight to London). Is her English superior to yours? Can she convert your indecipherable and incomprehensible thoughts into something coherent and can she dress up your drafts?

Or is she 50 plus, with a strong regional accent, a big *bindi* on her forehead and a bottom line bigger than the rest of her construction? Of course, if you are a finance person, you might settle for a big bottom line but on a personal level, I believe that if you take care of the top, the bottom will take care of itself.

What is her utility factor after working hours? If you can't read signals in these things, you are dumb anyway and therefore, don't deserve any better.

What is the size of your cell phone? Can it take pictures? Can it send and receive emails while you are sitting in your car? Has it global, national or regional roaming facilities? Do you have one or more than one? Is the hardware the latest available in the international market, or the one picked up off the shelf? The answer to these questions and all others will determine your scalability on the winding corporate staircase.

What is the size of your car? A car in the corporate world is not *just* a car. It is a corporate statement about you and your status. Is it a large one, mid-sized or is it an entry-level vehicle. Who drives it? You, or your chauffeur? Do you have one exclusively for your family? That will determine whether you are an also-ran corporate commodity or a rising star on the corporate horizon.

What is the size of your office? If, after 20 years of service, you are still in a 12/12 ft crummy hole, you don't count for much. You see, size matters. How does it compare with your colleagues? It is not just the size but the location. What is the view from your window? What about the furnishings, and the size of the table?

What is the location of your office vis-à-vis that of the boss? Can he drop in, holding his mug of coffee to have a chat with you, or does he prefer to have a long-distance intercom conversation with you? How often does he meet you? You can also check your status on the tea count. Is it served to you by the office boy without your asking for it? If you are asked and served, your status is of a passable quality. None of these privileges means that the next list of voluntary retirement scheme candidates has your name written on it.

How does your boss address you? By your pet name or your surname? Permit me to cite my example as an illustration. If the boss called me 'Prince', I knew I was sailing. If he called me 'DK', things were OK, by and large, that is. If it was 'Dinesh', I knew it was a borderline case. If I was called 'Kumar', things were really bad for me. The situation was always fluid and dynamic, according to the mood and the perspective of the only man (or woman) that counts.

How big is the gap between your seeking an appointment and getting it? You will get the first signal by the kind of response you get from the secretary. If she puts you on hold while she finishes her chat with her boyfriend on the other telephone, you have zero status. If it takes you three days to meet your boss, start applying for a job somewhere else. There is not much future here for you, particularly when you have to wait in the lounge after getting a firm appointment. You are a nix in the eyes of all those who see you twiddling your thumbs, seated on a low sofa in the waiting room. Your future is directly proportional to your accessibility to your boss, during and after working hours. Are you asked to stay on while he is discussing matters with others? That indicates that he has confidence in you and he would want to have your views on the subjects under discussion.

What is the size (i.e., colour) of your card(s)? Do you have one, or do you have many? Is it gold, silver, platinum, or just plain white? If you have none, you are nothing. If you have one, you are a little someone. If you have two, you are just becoming someone. If you have more than two and they are all gold (or platinum) cards, I might want to be introduced to you and introduce you to others.

What is the size of your computer? Meaning is it just a plain vanilla PC or do you have a state of the art Sony VIAO laptop or Apple iMac gleaming at you from your table? In this case smaller and sleeker is better!

What is the number of club memberships you hold? It is only the 'arrived' executive who is offered membership in the top-notch clubs of the city and the country. If you are still spending Sunday afternoons in Malleshwaram Club signing your own beer, while your colleagues are teeing off at the golf club at the company expense, you do not have to look far to determine your status. You will be lucky if you make the list of those who are on the super-annuating category. The kind of hotel accommodations you are entitled to is as important as club memberships. What kind of car comes to receive you at the airport, or are you still hailing a pre-paid taxi? Do you travel cattle class or club class?

When your customers, your colleagues, your bankers, and your business associates come calling on you, they will be looking for these visible signs.

People judge your products/services by the quality and reliability of the service that these provide. There are known parameters of functionality and aesthetics. Similarly, there are known parameters of how far you will go in the corporate world, some of which I have described above. Pay attention to these parameters more than you pay for your products and services.

Because it is only happy, and contented executives, whose physical, security, social and ego needs have been satisfied, and who are at the threshold of self-actualisation, (on my friend, Maslow's scale) who can produce good goods.

This Vision Thing 19

J IMMY NAGARWALA of Kibuta Steel is a no-nonsense, result-oriented person with a passion for new ideas. He is a man who is always in a tearing hurry. He sets a scorching pace for his people. That leaves him with enough time to mull over strategies. Like the crash course in total quality control that was discussed earlier. This time, let us take a peep into his day at work.

Jimmy Nagarwala has recently attended a workshop conducted by an internationally renowned management guru on the importance of creating vision statements for organisations.

He calls his secretary on the cell phone to assemble his senior people in the boardroom. He knows that with some quick thinking, he will be able to put together a vision statement while driving to the office.

By the time he reaches the boardroom, his top management team is already there.

The team knows that this meeting is going to be different. His second-in-command has just left his resignation letter at Jimmy *sahib*'s table because he can't take any more of his behaviour.

Jimmy enters the room like a man with a purpose and starts the meeting.

Gentlemen,

I have just come back from a workshop. It was explained to us that if we don't know where we are going, we will not get anywhere. A company must have a vision of its future. A company without a vision is like a ship without a destination.

I don't know how we missed this important aspect and, therefore, on the way back from the industry meeting, I made a vision statement.

He clears his throat and begins to read it with aplomb as if he were making the Gettysburg address. Only his strong accent gives him away. He reads out the mission statement as follows:

Kibuta steel will endeavour to be the best in the field of activity it is engaged in from time to time.

We will give our best to our customers, for it is on their goodwill on which our future depends.

Our people are our biggest asset and we will nurture them to the best of our ability.

Last but not the least, we will not, any longer, take out
of the community more than what we put into it.

Pam, the communications and extra-curricular activities manager, jumps for joy hearing these pearls of wisdom her boss has just stated. All the others resent her presence because she is the only manager on the committee of management (COM), the top policy-making body of the company.

The boss man rubs his hands in glee, and gives an indication that he is ready to field any doubts/ questions.

The executive vice president (EVP) is the first to respond.

'What are you raving about, Pam? This could be anyone's vision statement—from a cobbler's to a corporation's!'

Jimmy *sahib* goes red in the face. An attack on Pam is an attack on him.

'What do you mean? I have covered everyone he told us to cover. I have covered our customers, our people and our community,' Jimmy *sahib* says, angrily.

'Yes generally, but I thought the speaker would have mentioned that for the vision statement to be successful, it has to be specific to us. It has to be comprehensive and detailed. It is not meant to be a general statement of intention,' persists the EVP.

'I thought that I would give you the bare-bones version, the skeleton, for you all to put some flesh and blood and give focus to it. You know what I mean!' Jimmy looks pleased with the skeleton and bone analogy.

'For us to even give a try, we need to know first where we are going,' demands the EVP.

The senior vice-president (HRD) winks at the EVP and takes over. He has the most difficult task in explaining his boss's contradictory policies to everyone.

'Sir, in my previous company, it took us one full year to freeze our vision statement. First, we all had to sit down and make a draft, then take it down to the rank and file of the company, get their buy-in, incorporate their thoughts and then make it public.' Everyone knows that the guy is being mockingly reverent, because he is the real joker of the pack.

'Why should it take one year? You know we do things fast here. No, no, we don't have much time to lose,' persists the boss.

The EVP knows that it is time for him to take charge once again and he lets his impatience be known.

'A vision statement should detail what, where, how, who and by when all our objectives will be met. The one that you have given could fit General Electric and it could fit our copper supplier.'

'Yes, yes. It was something like that the speaker was saying,' says Jimmy *sahib*.

'It must be of special significance to our people and our customers. It should inspire our people,' added the HRD with mock reverence.

'Exactly,' the boss interrupted. 'It was exactly what we were told in the morning, that it should represent a compelling image of the future, and our vision should powerfully enable us to realise our dreams.' The boss was reading his notes verbatim.

The EVP and the HRD guy looked pleased as punch, having scored a point.

The R&D man always said something that made sense and therefore everyone took him seriously.

'I am always confused about the difference between the company's vision and company values. I mean what are we taking about here? Vision or values?'

The boss man is stumped because he had always held that, 'Value *shalue* and business don't go together. Even in America they are having trouble these days keeping to any values.'

The finance director, who is the boss's favourite, always keeps his mouth shut during meetings. His forte lies in producing figures of accounts to suit the occasion. One for the board, another for his MD, and yet another for the internal consumption of all the others. Besides, silence makes him look wiser than he really is. He chips in with his piece: 'Values are for monks. We are in business and we should not forget that basic thing.'

The EVP is angry at the finance man, who never signs any paper, never takes responsibility but spends most of the time with the boss, involved in some secret scheme or the other. He is in no hurry to let go.

'Values, we know, do not mean much to you but they are important. Values are incorporated in the vision. Vision is based on values but values cannot give you direction. Only vision can. It is the role of the vision to determine your destination. That is, if we get down to knowing where we are going from here.'

The finance man has a thick skin. Nothing bothers him. He has that superior-than-thou grin perpetually on his face.

'Unfortunately my calendar is pretty full till the end of the year. Why don't you guys sit down and complete the exercise? Pam here knows my views on all these and other policy matters, She can always represent me in the meetings when I am not there.'

It is on these occasions that the importance of being Pam is reinforced on all.

'Sure,' says the EVP, knowing that this initiative, like many others, will die a natural death.

'Sure,' says the HRD man assuringly, knowing that this was one more instance of wasted time.

'And don't forget, Pam, to get enough plaques with vision statements embossed on them. Have this year's diaries open with the vision statement.' The boss man instructs.

At this stage, his major-domo enters the room and says: '*Sahib*, Krishnan *sahib ne* golf course *se* telephone *kiya hai*'.

Everyone gets up as if on cue. But in less than a few seconds, Jimmy *sahib* is back and says, 'I am sorry I forgot to mention one thing that our speaker said. I thought it was rather cute. He said, "vision without action is merely a dream and action without vision is just pastime."'

The finance man and Pam follow the boss and the rest stay behind to re-enact the meeting. The mockingly reverent HRD man will now play the role of Jimmy *sahib* . . . .

Part III

Corporate Capers Miscellany

Aim is Fusion 20

MY PREFERRED pastime in the evening is sitting on a comfortable sofa at home, with a large drink in my hand, which has lots of ice in it. I then pick up a New Age book on enlightenment and ask my wife to press my legs, as shown in Indian movies. Of course, I get all of it except the last. She says, 'lead by example as you keep telling everyone who cares to listen'.

However, give me an invitation to a corporate party and I will drop that drink and rush there because that is where corporate excellence is at the peak of its performance. The aim of these parties is fusion between people and the bonding glue is not Fevicol but alcohol.

That is where the six-sigma quality comes into play, although at work, it may still be hovering around the four-sigma level. Quality at the workplace has waited so long, that a couple of years more are neither here nor there. In addition, the spirit of competition that is so important in the corporate sector is at its fieriest best when the occasion is the birthday bash of the boss or his spouse. That is one reason for my distinct penchant for corporate parties. The second is that you can slip in and out, and no one will know the difference. Many like me are there to make up the numbers. The boss's bashes have to be big!

I was talking of competition. It goes like this. If someone is trying to edge in with a wine and cheese party, he/she is going to be edged out in less than a week by a close friend who throws a champagne and strawberries event. If Goa beach is the theme of one party, the next host will transplant you to Bali though visuals, the dress code and music. I am hoping that one night soon there will be a Hawaiian party, where the dress code is grass skirts and bare tops (for men, I mean). Not being so daring in the matter of dressing, I will merge with the waiters behind the bar and spend most of my time enjoying the show from a vantage point. By the way, I have spent more interesting times with some waiters than with some CEOs.

The one price I have to pay for attending these grand events is the ear-splitting music that accompanies them, and the DJ's constant cajoling to come on to the dance floor. Dancing, as you might know, requires one left and one right foot to work in rhythmic co-ordination. However, in my case, as soon as I step on to the dance floor, I turn into either a two left-feet or a two-right feet animal. My feet decide the option at the last moment.

So, I stay out of trouble, until someone beautiful comes along and says, 'You want to dance with me?' I just melt out of humanitarianism and the sheer milk of kindness and let her cope with my limited skills. You know what I mean. This usually happens when the spirit level in the system is high.

Dancing is one thing that I find difficult to cope with, the other being all the kissing and hugging that happens at these dos. Women are hugging and kissing men, men are kissing and hugging women. Men are beginning to hug men. The young are hugging the old and the old are kissing the young. And I stand there like a deep freezer grunting away in the military style. In our genteel days, you acknowledged the presence of a lady by standing up if you were sitting down and bowed if you were standing up. At the last party, when someone came to kiss me, I just stood there like a tall date tree; completely unable to bend over for a kiss.

I am also amazed at the number of surprise parties that are held for corporate bosses. It must be a very dense one who cannot detect the feverish preparation that goes on for months before the party; or when guests are briefed where to park, how to tiptoe into the house, hide behind the cupboards (and in the bathrooms) while the lights are switched off. And then the celebrity (the boss) is led in, the lights are switched on and the cheerleaders start singing in the most monotonous and out-of tune voices, 'Happy birthday to you . . .'

I bet half of them want to shout, 'stop the drama and open the bar!' At least I do. I suspect that the guests like hiding behind the cupboards and under the beds with the lights off; otherwise there seems to be no rational explanation for this kind of show to survive so long.

But my favourite continues to be these all-inclusive, offshore, weekend parties at a holiday resort. I like the luxury of being picked up in a limo, driven to the spot of celebration for a decadent do that starts with dinner and ends with a champagne breakfast. You catch up on some sleep and are back by the poolside for a barbecue lunch. At these events, there are three to five and a half company people, depending on the size of the company, and the rest are friends and family (the half is the chief financial officer, who will be signing vouchers for my drinks and dinner).

The *coup de grace* is the birthday cake, which was so huge during one particular party that a dancer emerged from it when the birthday boy cut the cake and she did a cross between a belly dance and a Bollywood dance! This is when you get to witness corporate stamina—they never get tired celebrating!

Did I hear someone say that 'at this rate you will be taken off the party list'? I'm not too worried about that—they will be too busy reading Page Three to see what was written about their gala affair.

How to Conduct an Interview

21

S A consultant, you will receive many minor assignments that are really a waste of your time. For example, you might be called upon for a mid-term evaluation of MBA students, to assess the effectiveness of the training programme of the institution, and also to establish whether the assessment of the students by the external evaluators matches with that of the faculty or not.

This is a compulsory drill that business schools undertake, mainly to look good in the eyes of their students and be lauded for their fairness. But whenever there is an issue, the answer is invariably the same: 'You are right but the difficulty is that . . . .'

Similar to everything else that you do in life, there is a cost and there is a benefit. The benefit is that you are paid for two days of gas-potting but the cost is that you meet other so-called consultants, who are out to compete with you. The students do not get to say much because we try to teach them in 30 minutes what the faculty could not do in nine months.

Another such Britannia-like *Pastime* assignment is the job interviews. Though the final decisions are taken internally, they still want an *outside perspective* and *an independent, unbiased view*, so that if the candidate turns out to be a dud, well, you were there weren't you? The big chiefs will ask all the questions for which they may not know the answers but the idea is to impress the candidate of how far they have reached.

There are some sure-shot cases where I mark an X before the interviewee even starts uttering the first few words. The first category of candidates who report for the interview one hour before time, wait and fidget and smile at everyone who passes by. They make me feel so guilty for having made them wait, so I reject them for not valuing their time. How will they value mine if they can't take care of theirs? Time, we know, is money.

The second category are the ones who arrive late. Then they will tell you all about the awful Bangalore morning traffic that they had to wade through and therefore, the delay. I would have given them some chance if all they said was, 'I am sorry for arriving late', and left it at that. Saying sorry and then giving reasons for it, is not really saying sorry at all. So, I think that if you cannot commit to a time, can I really trust you with anything else? Why didn't you check the traffic conditions and plan your departure accordingly?

The third category includes those who send resumes that are like a 10-page story, with lots of 'I' did this and 'I' did that:

I was born in a humble agricultural home in a humble village near Udupi, a town famous for masala dosai and the best place to get them is Sirsi Tiffin Room near the bus stand. I studied in vernacular medium school. In the primary school, I represented my school in Kabaddi and our team was the runner-up at the Tehsil-level inter-school competition. I joined NCC and held the position of a lance naik. Although my family is from an agricultural background, by dint of sheer hard work, I came up in life and did my engineering in Tumkur. My ambition is to become the chief executive of a company and take it to higher and higher heights.

My hobbies include girl-gazing, daydreaming and TV surfing. My philosophy is to follow the footsteps of Mahatma Gandhi. I read Swami Vivekananda in my spare time. I

have clean habits. I am honest, hard working and sincere.
My father nurtured my ambitions and my mother taught
me high morals.

Great! But my dear man, I am asleep by the time I
have reached the finish line. I am not looking for a
marketing man who will bore the life out of his
customers, never mind your clean habits.

The fourth category attaches a number of
testimonials to their resumes. 'I have known this
candidate for the last 10 years. He is hard-working,
sincere and honest.' If you are hard-working sincere
and honest, why do you need people to recommend
you? If everyone is hard-working, sincere and honest,
why is white-collar crime going up? You spent your
last five years in Chennai while the person who
recommended you was rooted in Bangalore. How
was he in touch with your hard work, sincerity, and
honesty?

The finest example of such a testimonial was one
was written by a person with an English-sounding
name, which said, 'Mr Srinivas *says* that he is hard-
working, honest and sincere and he confirms that
he will do his utmost to deliver on the trust placed
in him.' I don't know whether he was displaying a
British sense of humour, or if this was his way of
getting rid of a pestering candidate who wanted a
testimonial from a foreigner.

The fifth category includes the candidates who
have read a book titled *Interviews Made Easy*, sub-
titled, *Ten Different Techniques to Sail Through the
Job Interview*. As the name implies, the book will
say that an interview is a two-way exchange of views.

So, feel free to ask questions, about the job, the
policies regarding promotions and anything else that
you need to know. After all, you are offering services
and skills that the company needs. There is an
exchange taking place. You are bringing value to the

table and, therefore, you have every right to ask. Besides, it will make you look like a person who knows his mind and who is sure of himself.

But this book is quite useless because it makes senior executives livid to be asked questions and they think, *you smart aleck, if you are being cheeky before I hire you, I don't know what questions you will ask after I hire you.* And some of you ask questions they don't know the answers to themselves!

But instead the senior executives will ask me, 'Do you have any questions or clarifications?' They ask you to look good and do not expect you to be taken seriously. What they are actually saying is, 'Your interview is over, now get the hell out of my sight. I am getting late for my next assignment.'

Just thank us and leave.

But on the other hand, if you are serious about the job, give me 10 good reasons why you think so and give me your reasons for telling me why you think that way (even eight are good enough but remember that it is the other guy who calls the final shot and it would be better for you to pay attention to him).

A Propensity for Verbosity 22

BEING A consultant has much compensation. The biggest of them is that you do not have to carry out any of your recommendations. Some other Joe Sucker has to do it, a kind of authority without responsibility. If he gets it right, 'see, you told him so'. If he gets it wrong, 'what did you expect him to achieve anyway?'

The results? You get to see the whole country at someone else's cost. Moreover, if the boss is the first person you see on arrival, and the last before departure, you can be sure that the HRD man will put you up in a deluxe hotel and approve your executive class travel. The sooner you are on a first-name basis with the CEO, the faster the upgrades in perquisites.

With your accumulated frequent traveller miles, you can even send your wife to your mother-in-law at no extra cost, and keep her there as long as you wish (tell her that there are only limited seats for the 'freebie' tickets anyway).

These, then, are the tangibles. The intangibles are free insights into the murky interiors of the corporate structure, or rather, the lack of it.

The last company I visited was thickly populated with people who were in the habit of using pompous, complicated, run-for-the-dictionary words. Their language was pickled in the *Random House Thesaurus*.

'The interpersonal quotient of this manager is low', actually meant, 'can't get along with his colleagues'. I am still trying to figure out what the HR manager meant when he said 'entrepreneurial propensity'. A rough guess is that it referred to his preference to meet new business challenges.

Propensity, by the way, is nothing but liking, preference, inclination or weakness. Have you noticed that bad habits rub off on us very easily? Soon, I found myself telling my wife that it looked to me that our children had acquired a propensity for dark chocolates!

During my next visit, the executive director knocked me off my feet when he said that they were deep into 'entrepreneurial dynamics and mediating structure between man and the society'. Words like 'managerial de-culturisation' were flying across the boardroom like rockets. I thought there would be some respite in the evenings. But I was wrong— these corporate heavyweights swirled their whiskies while simultaneously discussing 'perpetual and extended time horizons' and 'management-intensive approaches'.

In addition to the highly-polished written and spoken language they used, these executives were slowly but surely undergoing personality changes, albeit unconsciously. To match their propensity for long-winded conversation, encyclopedias and thesauruses began to occupy prominent places on their shelves.

They were not merely discussing problems, they were *addressing* them. I almost threw a paperweight at the manager who piped up to quote, 'The worst enemy of the best is not the worst but the good enough'.

I was convinced I needed a strong sedative when I heard that a team had been formed to study the configuration of performing relationships.

Back in the boss's room, I mentioned to him that this verbal disease was spreading like SAARS in his company. Surprised, he asked for my advice. I said, 'I don't know what you will do but I do know what Sir Winston Churchill would have done in similar circumstances. He would have confined them to barracks until each one signed an indemnity bond promising not to use any word bigger than four letters in written and/or oral communication.'

'But that is very limiting. I mean, just four-letter words?', argued the CEO *sahib*.

I said, 'It will send a strong message'.

I then told the boss man how Sir Winston had disciplined his verbose generals by insisting that he would throw out any report that was more than a page long. He also told them their reports better be precise, clear, and simple. He also insisted that they be logical and relevant. It was much easier to face Rommel than Churchill!

Somehow, Churchill's example went home because the boss promptly called his secretary and dictated the following memo to the heads of departments.

> *With immediate effect, the use of simple, conversational language will be encouraged in this company, both in written and oral communication. Thesauruses bought on the company's cost would be used to look for simple words. I will want to see some immediate results in this regard.*

I complimented him on the concise and clear message in his memo but suggested that the words 'in this regard' were unnecessary because the context was clear.

One more step stemmed the rot: the addition of this requirement in the annual confidential report. Simplicity of language used was added as an essential attribute for all managers.

Reflecting on the issue, I could not help but put some blame on the community to which I belong. We think it is our USP to make our language extraordinary. We are consultants, after all. It follows that our language cannot be run-of-the mill, used by everyone else! So, consultants will do what they want to do. However, why do working managers have to adopt complicated language to make an impression? My argument is that we can get along famously without torturing ourselves and others, with the use of tongue-twisting language.

'Life is difficult', is the first line in Scott M. Peck's famous book *The Road Less Travelled*. Let us not superimpose verbal complexity on it.

I miss my airforce days, when simplicity of words was exercised by all—'Roger' meant, 'I have received and understood your message'; 'Wilco' meant, 'I have received your message and will comply with it'; and 'Tally-ho' meant, 'I have spotted the target and I am going in for it'.

Tally-ho! Go for it—use simple language!

Bruised by Branding 23

ONE MORNING, while I was shaving with my Mach 3 Gillette blade, it occurred to me (going by the cuts on my chin!) how badly I had been used by brands. Financially speaking, no single disaster has struck me with greater ferocity than branding. Today, brands control me from top to toe; they have become the epicentre of my personality. I am not merely DINESH KUMAR. I am branded DINESH KUMAR—and at what a high cost! The vicious circle of brands is so overwhelming that I need to break out, or become broke. There just isn't another choice!

I recalled with fondness the good old days of 7 O' Clock blades when I spent only a minuscule part of the monthly budget on shaving—till Machs and then Super Machs came along, moving me from a state of rationality to irrationality. I am no longer in control—the brand managers/ambassadors are. The cost per shave has gone up logarithmically. But here I am, drooling over the brand name just because I have seen some inane advertisement on TV, which has a male model rubbing his chin in imaginary ecstasy, while a scantily-clad female model gives him come-hither looks.

Within the confines of my bathroom, I have often wondered what went wrong with using that erstwhile favourite, Old Spice, which attracted the opposite sex with greater intensity than the very expensive Hugo Boss *eau de toilette*, natural spray *vaporisateur*. I am convinced that it is nothing but a branding trick that is making deep holes in my pocket, with no extra mileage gained, vis-à-vis the female fatality factor. I don't even know what *vaporisateur* means, yet, I pay unearthly sums for it!

The same story applies to the change from a big unbranded jar of hair cream to the Brylcreems of today, which come in attractive red and green packaging, are heavily advertised, and totally subsidised by the likes of me.

When I am riding along the cycle of maturity, I know that a car is a mere machine designed to take me from point A to point B. And I need just one seat of the four in it to provide me with the means of mobility. Then along comes a Shah Rukh Khan, who drives me to such levels of insanity that I drive to my bank to take a loan to move from a Santro to an Accent. And before I have even done the third free servicing, he is pitching in for a Sonata, as he promotes the monogrammed car to be the ultimate symbol of luxury. I am hoping that I will not fall in his trap a second time! Before the advent of famous brand ambassadors, we were perfectly responsible people. Now they're trying their best to make us irresponsible and financially imprudent. Before the brand wars, like many other people, I never touched my capital and always lived on the interest it earned me. Today I am living in a state of perpetual debt.

Once you are trapped in the brand box, there is no easy way out. What would it look like if I walked out of my mega-bucks car in an ordinary, unbranded T-shirt? Only a Lacoste would do! So of course, it is not done to then drink rum at home (with the fancy car in my garage?); nothing less than Black Label scotch will be acceptable, out of the finest (branded) crystal tumblers of course! And so on—one brand leading to the acquisition of another. To do anything less would mean pitying glances from people who would say all kinds of things about me!

The other day, I went shopping for a new pair of jogging shoes. I needed a well-cushioned, springy and comfortable pair, which would not harm my knees and sprain my joints. I found exactly what I had been looking for, and the price was well within my budget too. It was then that the 'brand music' started to play in the back of my mind. So, I went to the nearest Nike shop and bought an expensive pair of trainers, which, of course, no one can even see in the early morning darkness. What else is this behaviour, if not brand mania?

I fervently hope that this obsession with brands stays at this level. But I have friends who tell me that 'it does not look nice' to have my hair cut by the roadside barber, whom I have been patronizing for the last 30 years. It is not done, I am told repeatedly. I also must have a manicurist, pedicurist and a hair stylist to match the brand equity I am associated with now. So, they are trying to persuade me to enrol in the high-end hair salon that is shortly opening in Bangalore. If I am still with the local barber, it is because he takes good care to update me on the (mostly raunchy) neighbourhood gossip. The service, including the tip, is not more than Rs 40. But I know that one day, I will have to make the shift to a well-appointed, air-conditioned salon, in a five-star setting.

The old adage that a man is known by the company he keeps is of no relevance any longer. The current ground reality is, that a man is known by the brand he sports. In this context, a man includes a woman. To be more specific, the woman includes the man!

What is the use of being a branded man if the wife is wearing silver jewellery? It cannot be a bottle of Hugo Boss for one and cheap perfume for the other! There will be no mix in that kind of match. Welcome to the world of the branded family. So, it is time for Tanishq to enter your home—designer jewellery and watches for the lady!

Watches and pens are my brand new brand worry. After having read that Mont Blanc and Rolex have opened exclusive showrooms across India, I have spent sleepless nights driving the idea of acquiring these accessories (at great personal cost) out of my mind. I am well aware that I have this nasty habit of leaving my pen all over the place, and that it would be only a matter of days before I lost such an expensive watch or pen. But the strong pull of the brand is driving me round the bend. Before I know it, I will be driving to the showroom and signing for them on my credit card!

Instead, I meet my dear friend, the CEO of a multinational company, to seek his advice about my brand sickness, hoping for some empathy but none is forthcoming. He keeps playing with his branded tie as he tells me that without brands, I would be part of the milling crowd—an insignificant nobody. Brands attract, he says. Brands are the driving force; the discriminating factor between haves and have-nots. 'You need to play in your league', he counsels.

So, that is the stage I seem to be stuck at—with no light at the end of the tunnel. When the telephone rings and the credit card company reminds me of the overdue that needs to be cleared.

I hope I don't have to acquire a new brand equity—indebted, and wearing a kurta, pyjama, and a pair of Kolhapuri chappals.

The Road to the Top is Paved with Villains 24

I s THAT really your belief? Your reality? Your experience? Are you sure that there are people out there, ready to stab you in the back given the first opportunity to get to the top? And if you don't stab them and cut them into pieces, will they make mincemeat out of you?

My experience has been different but then, that is my reality. Who am I to judge yours? According to you, the road to the top is paved with villains and to get there you have to either demolish them or be demolished. Right?

And what do you think you would you have to do, to get to the top, when the route up there is strewn with villains?

I suppose I will have to be a bigger villain. I will have to keep my saw sharpened.

And how do you think you can be a bigger villain?
That is where I want your advice.

That is a tricky one. I have not consulted in this area but going by experience, I can provide you with a broad approach:

1. *Never treat people as people:* If you treat people well, there is no hope at all for you to reach the top. Treat people as objects, as a dispensable commodity and when these objects have outlived their utility, pass them through your shredder like your old documents. Let a thousand flowers of selfishness bloom in you. Remember, you cannot make an omelette without breaking an egg! And you cannot reach the top without roasting a few villainous hides.

2. *Treat yourself as the epicentre of this world:* Shed the belief that the world rotates along its axis. It used to. Not any longer. The earth rotates around *your* axis. You can tilt it any which way you like and in the process of this rotation, if some people fall of by the wayside due to centrifugal forces, so be it. Remember, bosses with villainy flowing through their veins, nay, their very pores and cells, never shed a tear in grieving over a loss. Those mundane emotions are for weaklings like me. You are made of different mettle.

3. *Learn to insult with excellence:* To others, I advise complimenting in public and criticising in private. Sometimes, I even advise people to critique in private. People do not like being criticised in private any more. To you I would say, go forth my villain, insult loudly and clearly anyone who comes your way by saying something like, 'Is this a project report or a can of worms? My third-grade daughter could have done better than that!'. And, if the minor villain squirms, tell him to shave his twirling moustache and act like a man. Visit the website of The School for Scoundrels every night before going to sleep and pick up a few fresh insulting quotes that will take people by surprise. As far as praise is concerned, don't ever use it, otherwise you might be mistaken for a split personality.

4. *Remember it is not your greed but your entitlement:* You are the boss of your department. You work so hard. You bring value to the table. Today's times are not those of simple employment between an employer and an employee. They also refer to the exchange of value between you and the chief villain, who signs your monthly cheque. Villains are normally very generous with themselves and miserly with others. You save money for the company. Where will the company be without your hard work? What

is wrong then if you commit a minor act of delinquency by making something on the side? Remember, you are going to need the funds to get other smaller villains dealt with by your hatchet men. Their palms would need to be kept greased, at least until the time they are eliminated...

5. *Secrecy is the key:* Remain hidden. The best villains are those who are not visible; only their acts are. Through secrecy, you can act swiftly before the enemy on the way knows what hit him. In the armed forces, we were taught that the number one principle of war was surprise. So, remain secretive and surprise your enemy.

Cause pain while striking out at them. Make your favourite film villain your role model.

6. *To hell with them:* That must be your attitude. To hell with everyone but yourself. You should convey this with not only your attitude but also your expression. If you see someone in the morning and he or she wishes you good morning, your reply should invariably be, 'To hell with you. What is so bloody good about the morning? And will you move your ass and get out of my way!' That is the way to deal with villains while trekking to the top.

7. *Tell lies of Himalayan Olympian proportions:* Small villains are economic with the truth. Chief villains thrive on telling gigantic lies. They tell lies on paper and in person. Some call these lies harmless. For instance, my wife has been using a cream that promises the user she will become fair and lovely, from the day it was launched and it has not made an iota of a difference. If anything, she has gone a few shades darker. So, if big companies can lie on television, why can't you tell big lies in the privacy of the company you work in? Don't our political leaders tell white lies after being caught on camera in all kinds of suspicious situations involving large

currency notes? Use their vocabulary. Or, call it a 'corporate vendetta' if you are foolish enough to be caught on camera.

8. *Cut at the very roots:* All villains have their sidekicks. Eliminate them one by one. Now that is called striking at the roots. Leaders need followers to be leaders, even the villainous variety. Hanuman was great because he had a large army of monkeys to follow him. Do you think he could have destroyed Lanka without them? The same principle is applied here. The only way to deal with villains is to destroy their *bandars* gross by gross.

9. *Stock your cellar with the vintage stuff:* One of the weaknesses of villains is that they like to drink. And to show off, they keep the whole bottle on the table. You must have seen this in Hindi movies. Next to the bottle you will find only a glass. No soda, no water. They drink the stuff neat. Give it to them on weekdays and weekends. Let them stay in a perpetual stupor. When you are stabbing them in the back, they will not know the pain. Remember that alcohol is the best painkiller (as you must know from personal experience).

10. *Swift revenge is the key:* If a villain on the way up acts up or acts against your interest, go for the jugular, or *veina jugularis* as they say in Latin. Let the act of revenge be merciless, swift and complete. There are no halfway measures in villainy. Either you are doing *dhishum dhishum* to someone, or he is doing *dhishum dhishum* to you. Which do you prefer? By now, you should not have any doubt.

These, chief villain, are the 10 commandments of villainy on the way to the top, littered with the corpses of enemies, who don't even deserve indecent burials.

Can you feel some negative energy in the room? No? Then, you've graduated with flying colours.

Five Good Reasons why we have Consultants

CONSULTANTS ARE consultants because they have no other choice but to become consultants. In all the cases I have studied, including my own, I have concluded that there are five major reasons why consultants choose their profession. Of course, there are many other minor reasons like proven track-records, specialities in subjects like mergers and acquisitions, and total quality. Given below are, however, the compelling reasons to become a consultant:

1. You desperately need a business card. You need an identity. Imagine meeting a corporate bigwig in a social setting, who asks you for your business card and you have to say that you have none, or take out one where you have scribbled *formerly managing director.* You can be sure that the conversation will stop there itself. Nobody wants to talk to a has-been. Even if you are dressed up in a pinstripe suit. On the other hand, if you were to present a professionally designed card which has a company logo and a vision/mission statement, embossed with elegantly raised letters, what an impression it would make!

2. The second compelling reason is that there cannot be two managing directors/managers under one roof. One present and the other, former. There are bound to be inter-department rivalries. I can best explain this

with an example. Suppose you are indifferent to food, whether it was cooked minutes before, or days before, you would start giving lectures on economy of scales. *I just don't understand why the driver or you have to go shopping every day. Buy your rations for a month and vegetables and fruits for a week and be done with it. Or, what is the difficulty in cooking for three or four days and storing it in the freezer? Besides the economy of scales, we have to keep economy of effort in mind.*

On the other hand, if you are a fussy eater, you might start singing the praises of Just-in-Time (JIT) Larder Management inventory. Your language will, of course, be different. *It is a golden principle that you must buy on a need basis. That is how the Japanese became globally competitive. It is always the pull strategy. When you need it, pull it from the market and keep the inventory low. Work for zero inventories.* Either way, the present managing director is going to tell the former, *shut up and mind your own business.*

3. To stave off depression. You have been used to freebies. You have been used to free travel and patronizing the finest restaurants. You have seen the world. You have enjoyed enormous privileges and perks, and if you think you can get into a Buddha-like state straightaway, think again. You will be miserable. Time will hang on you (see 'Partings are Painful' in this book for more details).

4. You need a regular revenue stream. What used to be a regular income before is now termed the revenue stream. That is the major difference between a professional and a consultant. Verbosity. Without a regular revenue stream,

you will find it extremely difficult to maintain your self-esteem. There is also the real danger that your spouse will also suffer from psychological scars when he/she doesn't find any pay in your bank statement. In any case, instead of getting a cup of tea in bed, you will now be making tea for your spouse. Do you want to reduce yourself to such a degrading and pitiable state? Think hard. The choice is yours.

5. You will otherwise end up as a postal clerk. This needs to be explained further. After a year or so of retirement (and sometimes even earlier), you will become an errand boy for the family. Either answering the telephone or as the grocery man. Don't be surprised if your daughter-in-law (DIL) rings you up and says sweetly: 'Papa, I was wondering whether you would be able to courier this little packet to Delhi to my mother. You know Papa, these children are driving me crazy, and I just don't have time. And while you are at it, can you also deposit a couple of cheques at the bank?' Now, out of sheer guilt that your grandchildren are driving your DIL crazy you will accept the assignment, and you can't even say you are busy. Busy doing what?

Ten Good Reasons Not to Hire Consultants

1. They always sing one song—about downsizing, restructuring, and cost cutting. In this process, no one is free from the firing line. Everyone is expendable. Why should you be fool enough to put your necks on the chopping block for someone who doesn't know a thing about your business? As it is, their information is so outdated that they

first have to *capture* the latest from us, rephrase and paraphrase it, and then dish it back to us in the most unintelligible manner.

2. They will end up creating a great divide, isolating us from our bosses by feeding them with all kind of things that have been superficially picked up in bits and pieces. There will be some who will fawn over you during coffee breaks, prodding you to act on some half-baked information. The blamers and complainers will get the upper hand.

3. We don't like people who have the authority to suggest changes but take no responsibility for all the blood-letting and blood-spilling that will follow. If consultants are that smart, why don't they join our company and sweat it out with us? Why don't they become internal mentors instead of being fly-by-night operators?

4. They charge too much. Let's be frank. Consultants believe that their value will be directly proportional to the cost we incur on them but the truth is, we don't like signing fat cheques for one day's effort, for amounts equal to our ten days' pay.

5. They go away after conducting a three-day workshop, during which our backlog is piling up. We will be spending three weekends to catch up on this work besides which, our families resent the time spent away from them.

6. There is a lot of gas-potting they do. Words flow out of them so lucidly and glibly that we are all impressed. When we reach home and our wives ask us what was taught to us, we find ourselves saying *come to think of it, I don't remember anything worthwhile.*

7. They are movers and shakers. They keep saying *this organisation needs a shake-up* or, *this organisation has become complacent*. We like making small corrections on a daily and weekly basis, depending on the feedback and our experiences. We don't like high revolution churning.
8. Our experience shows that consultants will take us around a full circle and we will arrive at the same platform from where we boarded, a kind of back-to-square-one situation.
9. When the plans they suggest are found to backfire, they will be nowhere to be found, quite likely consulting with someone else.
10. There is also the abundant possibility that they will suggest sacking the CEO and take his place.

And finally, if consultants are as smart about waste reduction as they keep telling us, then let us go 50:50 on the gains when accrued.

But that's never acceptable to them.

A *Deadly Disease* called *Founderitis* 26

SOCIAL SCIENTISTS have this insatiable urge to study human behaviour, often of the most ludicrous variety. The other day I read that social scientists in the UK had been able to establish a direct correlation in the rise of love making in automobiles to the rise in ambient temperature.

There was also a report that a fair percentage of women preferred to own a fridge to having a husband. If I am right, the same study said that some woman were quite willing to exchange their second-hand husbands for brand new fridges!

In fact, after my family members read this report, I came quite close to being exchanged for a fridge. Fortunately, the size of the fridge offered in exchange was too small to meet the needs of our large family and I stayed kept. But this chapter is not about husband–fridge exchange programmes.

Rather it is about my concern regarding the priorities of these social scientists! Why have these chaps found no time to study an incurable disease called founderitis; to my mind it is a deadly disease that kills organisations, profit making or non-profit making. This organisational disease is worse than diabetes, which I am told, sometimes spares a whole generation. Foundertis shows no such discrimination. So, it is left to a novice social observer like me to launch the study on this disease.

I have observed that this incurable disease largely strikes family businesses. Fortunately, the symptoms of the disease are all too visible for further study.

The first symptom is when you send a negative feedback on the products or services provided by the afflicted organisations, it is taken as a personal attack on the family. For example, if it turns out that the cement sold by Kumar Cement Limited is of poor quality, such a report will be read as Person Kumar is of poor quality and a defensive tirade will start, even at the cost of losing the customer.

The second symptom is that it will be claimed that the offspring, who are in their early twenties and have just returned from MIT or some other business school of repute, are being put through their paces. 'I have told my son that he has to go through the grind of working on the shop floor; dirty his hands like everyone else before he can lay a claim for any job.' These statements will be loudly made in the office and at cocktail parties. 'I have made clear to him that there are no free lunches in life' or, 'Just because I am a majority owner doesn't mean that the next generation will automatically get into the driver's seat.'

The truth is somewhat different. The young fellow wearing a 110-dollar tie and a suit costing over 500 dollars, will swagger out of a Merc, which will be parked right in front of his office. Not the right outfit to dirty your hands in, is it? On arrival, everyone would be ready to vacate the seat for the 22-year old, who would accept the invitation on the third day. By the tenth day, the blue-blooded scion will be making sweeping changes without any regard to the combined experience of the many people who have served the organisation from the time he was in his nappies.

When the case study formula taught in the business does not work for the youngster, he will start complaining to the family head that everyone in the company was resisting change. These people have become too complacent and set in their work attitude. In less than a year, he will be given independent charge of a department which took others at least a decade to master. This is what is meant by 'dirtying hands' and 'going through the mill to gain experience'.

Soon, he will start attending the company's Board meetings as an invitee and will be treated with deference by the directors of the founderitis-afflicted company. Deference comes naturally to the directors because it is all that a captive Board of such a company knows for peaceful co-existence.

His designation may be assistant manager but his word is respected by the vice-presidents. He get to fly to his alma mater by first class for the annual reunion.

As the number of siblings increase, it will lead to fragmentation of the company because no one but no one will accept the position of a deputy. Moreover, with time, the pieces of cake will be so small that the competition will begin to swallow them one by one. Where does this disease finally lead? Well, it is a near fatal disease. In three or four generations, the organisation dies a slow death. In such a company, total control of a near-dead company is better than minority control of a healthy and vibrant one.

Having studied commercial organisations through the eyes of a lay social scientist, let us see how it affects non-profit organisations and what the symptoms are there:

The founders are extremely nice; a polite, affable and friendly lot till the followers stay followers and don't entertain any thought even in their dreams of a leadership role.

- Their teams consist of boneless wonders, who are happy living in reflected glory.
- Their medium-term plan is to minimise the influence of the co-founders, the long-term goal being to eliminate them.
- They spend a lot of time networking, double talking, creating politics, gossiping and manipulating. Their telephone bills are usually very high but they consider the return on investment worthwhile.
- They are not above changing the company's rules and regulations to maintain their commanding heights.
- If unfortunately, or by some negligence they lose their prime position, they fight back with a determination matching Taliban fighters.

- When their term expires statutorily, they usually appoint their spouse in the Laloo *bhai* style.
- They use the institutional platform for self-serving purposes.
- They are not above spreading rumours about the non-cronies.
- They maintain good relations in high places for just-in-case situations.
- They are very hard working and spend time on their mission to the exclusion of all else in their lives.
- They like people who are gifted with the ability to raise their hands to the motion and who do it fast.
- They are good PR people who maintain good relations with the media and are generally seen from a distance as paragons of virtue and selflessness.
- They generally possess a high IQ but are not really up on EQ.
- They cry easily to win sympathy votes.
- Before anyone can say 'no' to their proposal, they are apt to say promptly that since no one is against the motion the same is passed unanimously.
- They like fund collection and fund collectors.

This is but the first draft of a pilot study done by the author who is now looking for sponsorship to continue the study in depth. Once we can establish the genetic build-up of this deadly disease, there is great hope to eradicate it, or at least contain it from spreading. Any observations are also welcome.

A
D
E
A
D
L
Y

D
I
S
E
A
S
E

A Piece of Advice for Newbie Managers 27

D IGNITARIES ON the dais, dear parents, esteemed guests, members of the press, and my young friends:

As I was climbing the dais, a few thoughts were running through my mind. One of them was this: Why do ordinary mortals like my colleagues and I who are gracing the dais, become dignitaries just because we have climbed a height of say, three feet? I intend bringing this up during dinner with my colleagues later but by then, we will be back to our original ordinary status anyway.

The other thing that is a bit of a bother is this funny-looking rented black gown and hat that I am wearing. This hat is already giving me a massive headache. It is a wee bit smaller than the diameter of my head and it still has the not-so-pleasant odour of the last person who wore it. Then there is this mystery that I need to resolve. Why is one gown red and the others black, and why is one plume designed to fall over the right ear and the others on the left ear? I know these are insignificant things, or are they?

Young friends, it is an important day for you. I can see a glint in your eyes. Today you come to the end of a very expensive course and you are hoping that you will land a good job to justify the expense your parents have incurred. Given the job market situation, you and your parents do not have to worry. I can say with confidence that any smart person can land a job today.

Let us now get down to the business of today.

I am sure that you have applied to a number of companies for a job. Remember to speak when you are spoken to, and do not go throwing your newfound wisdom on the interviewer. Remember that most of them will not be MBAs, and that most of them think that MBAs are snooty sorts, who need to unlearn the many wrong things they have learnt in the B-schools. They are partly right and partly wrong. Let me discuss only those cases where I believe they are right.

You would have been, I am sure, given a heavy dose on leadership, with some case studies of successful leaders and others who are not so successful. You would have been told that leadership is contextual. That the same leader can be authoritarian in some circumstances, and participative or consensual in others. Also, that the leaders that you will meet and work under will not fit into any of the categories that you have been taught about. That is good learning but you will not have to use this knowledge for the next five years or more because you will be led and not be leading. Therefore, my advice is to forget about leadership and learn more about subordination. Yes, subordination.

For many years you will have to be content with carrying your boss's briefcase and take notes for him during meetings.

The B-schools, to the best of my knowledge do not offer a capsule on how to stop worrying and start managing your bosses. My advice to the schools would be that such a course should be introduced without any delay since many people have been badly bruised because they did not know how to manage their bosses effectively. Our young managers need to be taught the psychology of their bosses. For example, how to identify the mental make-up of their bosses. Do they reflect narcissist, or obsessive-compulsive behaviour? What are the main characteristics of such people and how do you deal with them with differentiation? The chances are that you may be working with downright psychopaths. So, do read a lot of psychological material. It will stand you in good stead.

I know there are going to be some amongst you who will be proud recipients this evening, of some trophy or the other. While I congratulate you, I'd like to caution you that while these trophies may help you land a job, it is not likely that you will be a CEO one day. The job of a CEO goes mostly to those who have a high EQ and team spirit, people who know their limitations and work within those limitations—not to those who win trophies. They are not shy of hiring those with a higher IQ to do the job for them. I am not making this up. The subject has been researched often enough, and the result of the various findings are, that more people with higher IQ work for those who have lower IQ and not the other way around. The research shows that smart guys cannot handle criticism or rejection and there is plenty of that in corporate life. Research also shows that those who sit in the middle rows in their class make better leaders than those who sit in the front. Well, if you have already done well, there is nothing we can do to reverse your fate.

Your director was telling me that this year, most of you have chosen to major in finance. That is a very good idea. It is a good idea to know the various ratios of finance, different methods of depreciation, cash flows and discounted cash flows. However, nobody would have taught you here how to fudge figurers without anyone getting wind of it. How to show higher or lower profits than actual figures; how to capitalise revenue expenses, or how to hoodwink banks to give you the loans you don't merit. I suppose that you do not have to worry too much about that. Your senior colleagues in the finance department will take you through the paces. Do not express shock at the not-so-legal manoeuvrings that take place. Everyone does it.

Another bit of practical advice. Dress well to show that you are a reasonably well-to-do person. Do it even if you are saving half your salary for your younger sister's wedding. As bankers give loans easily to those companies least needing it, in companies, promotions are given to those who appear to be economically comfortable.

Let me see if there is another piece of practical advice I can give you. Ah, yes. Do not become grooved in a speciality. In the beginning, you may not have a choice. You may have to specialise in marketing, finance or technology but get into the area of general management by seeking lateral shifts. That is my advice through personal experience. In the corporate world, it is better to know a little thing about everything than to know everything about a little thing. You can always get a specialist to do the detailing for you. So, move laterally and then vertically and so on.

The one thing you must never say is *This is how they taught us in the B-school*. The pure fundas of B-schools never work. They have to be tempered to suit local conditions, of which there are many.

And finally, young friends, stay excited about your futures. In your new world, excited people are valued, even if there is nothing to be excited about. Let the bosses say that 'this guy has some fire in his belly'. Remember, the adage 'fools rush in where angels fear to tread' does not work in the big corporate world.

That is all that I have to say on this very exciting day to both you and your proud parents. The road to work is paved with headhunters. Here is wishing you happy hunting.

Making up Your Mind on Your Mind

Y OU ARE an industry/business person. You are in the mood for self-analysis to determine to which Freudian psychological box you belong. Given below is an easy test, which does not need a therapist or require you to pay the high consultation fee shrinks charge these days. It also saves you the embarrassment of being seen in the company of a psychotherapist.

Please make sure you complete the test before looking at the results?

1.

(a) A media manager is necessary for a leader to manage your image.

(b) The PR department of the company should handle media and project the company as an entity.

(c) If you have something to say, you will get media attention anyway.

(d) None of the above.

2.

(a) Leaders are born.

(b) Leaders can be trained.

(c) If people love you enough and accept you, you will eventually emerge as a leader.

(d) None of the above.

3.

(a) You believe that the leaders should keep their own counsel on important issues.

(b) You make sure who you should trust and who you should not.

(c) You trust others because trust begets trust.

(d) None of the above.

4.

(a) *Do you think that one must dream unrealistic dreams and make them into reality?*

(b) *Do you believe that only realistic dreams can be converted to reality?*

(c) *Dreaming is a good thing for the leaders but you do not have to act upon all dreams.*

(d) *None of the above.*

5.

(a) *Audacious people make great leaders.*

(b) *Audacious people bite the dust.*

(c) *It is not through audacity that you get results but through enrolment of people.*

(d) *None of the above.*

6.

If you had time to read just one book, would you choose?

(a) *Autobiography of Jack Welch or some other great leader?*

(b) Seven Habits of Highly Effective People *by Stephen Covey?*

(c) *Try to read a bit from both.*

(d) *None of the above.*

7.

(a) *Would you call yourself.*

(b) *An dependent person?*

(c) *An interdependent person?*

(d) *None of the above.*

8.

If you had a choice:

(a) *You would have chosen your present role.*

(b) *You believe that consulting would have been a better choice.*

(c) *HR or social settings would have suited your personality.*

(d) *None of the above.*

9.

(a) *Do you see yourself as passionately directed?*

(b) *Directed by an inner compass?*

(c) *You believe that you are directed due to external factor.*

(d) *None of the above.*

10.

(a) *You want to see something solid in people for them to impress you.*

(b) *Incremental improvements are sufficient to impress you.*

(c) If you accept people as they are, they will go out of the way to do things to impress you.

(d) None of the above.

11.

(a) IQ is the most essential attribute of a leader.

(b) The right combination of IQ and EQ is needed.

(c) How far one will go in leadership will depend solely on your EQ.

(d) None of the above.

12.

(a) If people don't perform, fire them and hire suitable replacements.

(b) Help to train them to become better managers.

(c) Every person has an intrinsic worth; help them to find it and they will become better managers.

(d) None of the above.

13.

(a) Is charisma an essential attribute of a leader?

(b) Do you believe that charisma without teamwork will eventually fail?

(c) You believe that charisma, like beauty, is skin deep. Love is the essential ingredient.

(d) None of the above.

14.

(a) Do you ask the question 'Why not'?

(b) Do you ask question 'Why'?

(c) 'Why' or 'Why not' are two aggressive extreme positions which should be avoided.

(d) None of the above.

15.

(a) You consider oratory an essential attribute.

(b) Oratory would not be very high on your list.

(c) Oratory might sway people temporarily. You have to help people find meaning to their lives.

(d) None of the above.

16.

(a) Your space is private to you and you must guard it.

(b) This is something you will decide on each occasion.

(c) If you give space to others, others will give space to you.

(d) None of the above.

17.

(a) Emotions are for kids.

(b) Emotions, when appropriate, should be expressed.

(c) A person is the sum total of his/her emotions.

(d) None of the above.

18.

(a) Leadership is about invincibility.

(b) Self-confidence and self-esteem is important. Invincibility is not.

(c) Invincibility is the platform of the week.

(d) None of the above.

Let us now arrive at the answers. If you answered (*d*) in the majority of the questions, you belong to none of the three established types of personalities, given below:

You are mostly a weathercock, who sways with the wind as it blows. Some people may regard you as a wimp. You are probably in your position because you are a close relation of the boss or of the largest shareholder. On your own steam, it is not likely that your presence will be acknowledged or that you absence will be missed. It is your wife's way or highway and you don't count. Enjoy yourself as long as the good fortune lasts.

If, on the other hand, you answered (*a*) in the majority of cases, you are a narcissist, deeply in love and pathologically preoccupied with yourself. Your need to be admired is insatiable. You can make a great leader and cause a great amount of transformation in the company that you head. You are most likely highly distrustful and, therefore, disconnected emotionally from your people. Your narcissism will stand you in good stead but the danger is that there might come a time when you will begin to view yourself as larger than life and believe that the earth rotates on your axis. If that happens, you are heading for a self-destructive mode and will most likely end up in a state of ignominy. In that state, you might divorce your wife and marry your secretary. If you remain a productive narcissist, you are likely to retain good sense and walk away from your company with a hefty separation packet but the chances are that you will create a big mess in the succession plans.

If, most of your answers were (*b*) you are obsessive self-reliant and conscientious. You like to resolve conflicts and can handle crisis well. You are always trying to create win-win situations and focus on continuous improvements. You lack vision and daring though you are a good listener and a great coach. You will be directed by your morals. You will make a good leader but never a great one. You will play the game according to the rules and are very budget conscious.

If most of your answers fall in the (*c*) category, according to Freud, you are an Erotic personality type. Before you start dreaming of being the local Romeo, Freud did not mean erotic in the sexual sense. He meant that your need to love others and be loved is great. You are likely to depend on those who you fear will stop loving you. You are a good enabler and a helper. You avoid conflicts but are caring and supportive. You seek direction from outside of yourself. Helping others comes naturally to you. You will be a good consultant.

Having made up your mind on your mind, what lies next? If you want to be happy in your work and life, find a work situation that suits your personality type or stay put and be in a state of incongruency all your life.

But be warned—incongruency is the source of all life's problems!

Part IV

Buddha
on
Management

May You Find Peace 29

T HIS CHAPTER is for all the suffering *bhikshu*
(disciples) managers out there—may you
find peace! Life, unfortunately is all about
suffering. I refer in particular to corporate suffering,
my sermon for today.

The source of all suffering is desire. You suffer
either because you cannot get what you desire, or
because you get something that you don't. That is
the ultimate truth of all suffering, including the
corporate variety. When you get rid of desire, suffering is alleviated.

Another reason why people suffer is because they
agonise over the reality of a situation—for them,
that is their ultimate reality. My dear *bhikshus*,
that is your personal reality. The ultimate corporate reality is very different.

Not understanding this ultimate truth is ignorance, which is the source of all pain, suffering, and
strife. It is because of this ignorance that the corporate sector is inhibited with so many fractured souls,
living their managerial lives in vain, and in perpetual pain. If only you *bhikshus* understood that all
pain is avoidable!

I completely empathise with your pain, as I have
experienced it myself (until I rose to the top floor of
the corporate building, when I started causing it to
others). Enlightenment struck at the stroke of midnight, the night of my retirement, while returning
from my farewell party. Here are the nuggets of wisdom I received, during a Scotchy trance:

The first mantra of corporate reality, my dear
bhikshus, is that whatever may be the corporate

structure, lean or fat, top down or flat, hierarchical or fluid, there are only bosses and there are only underlings. And, in the ultimate analysis, there is, only one Boss, and all the intermediate bosses are also His underlings. Therefore, his reality is the real one; yours is only subjective.

The second mantra, young *bhikshus*, is when his reality conflicts with yours. He will reprimand you, get angry with you, leading to a lot of pain for you. If his reality matches yours, he will appreciate you, promote you and you will be happy. When neither of the above happens, you will be in a neutral state, a corporate nobody.

Now, dear *bhikshus*, we proceed to the next step, which takes place at the experiential level—the first phase of meditation.

All emotions of pain, joy and neutrality will manifest themselves as physical sensations. Pain will manifest as an unhappy sensation in your body. Joy will make you appear happy, and the neutral state will lead to a feeling of dullness taking over.

Your job is simply to observe these sensations as they come and go, without passing judgement. If you feel happy, don't cling to this sensation, just observe it. In the same way, if you feel pain or a feeling of dullness, don't try and get rid of these feelings, or even move away from them. You need to understand here that there are no good or bad sensations but merely impressions which you need to merely observe.

When you merely observe them without attaching any importance to them, you will find that they gradually lose their intensity and soon they will disappear. This is because nothing is permanent—whether it is life, pain, or happiness. That is the beginning of enlightenment. You are born to die in the corporate life so that you can be born again.

Now, if you observe these sensations on a regular basis, every time your boss praises you, causes you pain, or neglects you, you will learn to merely observe them and not react to any of these feelings. As a result, you will soon (within a year or so) become desensitised to such an extent that you will cease to create new corporate karma. If you go back to reacting you would have to face the consequences of the newly created karma.

You are finally on the path of corporate liberation. There will be many hurdles along this path, though. There will be days when the boss will praise you and you will want to run home and open a bottle of champagne—don't! Meditate on your inner self instead.

On some days, when your boss causes you pain, you will want to murder him. Sit at your desk instead and closely observe your breath. You will soon notice that all sensations dissipate. Surrender to the ultimate reality that your current boss is like the Buddha, the enlightened one. The rest is *maya*, an illusion.

Your ultimate goal is corporate liberation and through that, regular promotions. For that to happen, you must believe in the laws of impermanence and surrender to the higher power and the ultimate reality (your boss) and repeat to yourself, *this is my reality of this moment.*

Yes *bhikhshu,* you have a question?

Yes, Monk, I have a question. What should I do when my boss not only refuses to recognise the good work I am doing but also ridicules me in public and I can't take it any more?

You will experience this, not once but many times in your corporate life. Your job is not to create any new corporate karmas and ruin your life. If observing your breath or meditating on your inner self does not help in these dire circumstances, send him *meta bhavana*. Keep saying to him, *may you be happy! May you be liberated! May you realise your dreams!* Keep doing that until the storm blows over and you get back to the state of equanimity and peace.

You have another question, *bhikshu*?

If I carry on like this, I will reduce myself to a doormat!

Let me clarify, dear *bhikhshu*. You must be guided by your own experience. Don't take my word as the truth. That is *my* truth based on my experience: my cause, my effect; your cause, your effect. By the way, what are you in your company?

I am a senior engineer.

And how many years of service?

Almost 25 years.

Yes, *bhikshu*, your question?

What about the karma our bosses commit? Should they go scot-free? That will not be fair even in the corporate world!

I can best answer this with a couplet by Kabir, who said:

Kabira teri jhopadi gal katyan ke pass.

Karan ge jo bharan ge, tun kyon bhaya uddass.

(Oh Kabir, Your hut is next to the butcher.

He will suffer the consequences of his doings, why are you becoming sad.)

(The *bhikshus* thronged the monk and wanted to know when the next session would be, and what would be the subject. He replied that it would be on *awareness towards duty* and *equanimity towards results*. The ashram would email the date and time to them.

Then the monk watched as they left the *bhiksha* in a big basket near the exit of the hall. Some left Scotch bottles, some dry fruits, and others dropped in wine bottles, and fresh fruits, all charged to their expense account).

How to Stop Worrying and Start Managing

E VERY MANAGEMENT expert will tell you that it is as important to manage your bosses as it is to manage your subordinates. Apart from being able to manage yourself, of course. But do the business schools care? Not one of them has a capsule on 'How to Manage the Boss'. Not one. I believe that they short-change their students by neglecting this very important aspect of management education.

The results, naturally, are along expected lines. The MBA greenhorns land into the corporate world with a thud, and have no idea what is about to strike them. It will be quite a while before they come anywhere close to having subordinates but the need to manage their bosses will start on day one.

This is the first truth. The second is that you may get away with a carte blanche approach with your subordinates but if you try the same omnibus approach to your bosses, you've simply had it.

What is so unique about managing bosses? If it were not something special, the management guru, Peter Drucker, would not have written an essay on it.

The very first and most crucial step is to find out what kind of species you are dealing with. Let me explain this further:

1. *Detection:* The first step is to detect who the bosses are on your radarscope. You will find that there are many, some who appear direct, others indirect; some

who look like potential ones, and others who assume that they are your bosses, although they are not. The last category is important. They are usually the fast trackers who extend their jurisdiction, often without cause. You will have to learn to calibrate your responses to meet the differing demands of all these kinds of bosses.

2. *Identification and Engagement:* These are two of the most important steps and, therefore, I will explain them in greater detail. Your salvation lies in the correct diagnosis of the personality of all your bosses. Since they come in many forms and shapes, your interaction with them will depend on the kind of person you are dealing with at any given point of time. I have attempted to describe some of these below.

- *The Intellectual:* He is always reading one management book or the other; during flights; while being driven to and from work; and even on the toilet seat. He will be on a perpetual intellectual high but low on implementation. You will identify him by his language because he will mostly use unintelligible phrases picked up from the books he has read. And don't be surprised if his management dictums keep changing like the flavours of the month.

  Have patience to listen to him and say *wah wah* when he gives you a daily dose of wisdom before he begins any serious discussions. Also, be prepared to attend one training seminar or the other to try and match his knowledge.

- *The Mover and Shaker:* You will recognise him by his language. *This organisation needs a change. It needs a thorough shake-up. It has become too complacent.* He is continuously on the move, never satisfied with his life, his work, or the pace at which things are happening. Everyone except him moves too slowly for his liking. So his energy is spent shaking his subordinates and he ends up tired, frustrated and friendless.

Stay out of his way. Minimum engagement is the key.

- *The Road Rager:* A close relation to the above. He is the one who cannot wait for his car, the lift, or the traffic lights to turn green. He will rave and rant, and pace up and down if there is more than a 10 seconds delay in anything. His identity is totally tied with the instant satisfaction of his wishes. If the car arrives late at the airport, he sees that as the biggest degradation of his status.

  Ensure that all his requirements are met on time and that there are always standby arrangements in place.

- *The Dictatorial Boss:* It is either his way or the highway. There is no third option, no argument, and no discussion, much less the airing of facts. There are only his opinions and decisions. He can be polite to the extent of saying, 'Be reasonable, do it my way'. He is a road roller.

  Carry a notebook, jot down his instructions, word by word, and execute them like a faithful servant. 'Three bags full, sir', is your mantra.

- *The Procrastinator:* He will never take a decision. As he comes close to it, he will say *but on the other hand, if we do that then . . .* He is the 'ifs and buts' manager, the troubled soul and the perpetual fence-sitter.

  Have compassion for him, take decisions on his behalf, and make them sound as if they are his.

- *The Wheeler-Dealer:* He is always on the prowl to strike deals for his personal benefit. *A cut here, a commission there . . .*

  It is strictly your call. You can either lubricate his way in making his deals, or stay clear of him.

- *The Any-which-way Result-oriented:* His philosophy is getting results, any which way he can. The means are not important, the end is. *I want it done. I don't care how you do it,* is his vocabulary. Fair or foul, good or bad, honest or dishonest, anything goes. *We did not hire you to give excuses or justify failures,* is his reply to any difficulty that you might pose.

  Work your way in finding a new boss.

- *The Process-oriented:* This kind of boss is interested in results achieved through the right processes. He is the patient type, who wants to establish the right way of doing things because there are no shortcuts to achieve good results.

  Stick with him. He will appear slow. But often, slow is fast.

- *The Corporate Golfer:* He will harangue you to death with the minutest details of his last game. How he came from behind to catch up with the leader on the 17th hole. *That beautiful putt on the 15th*, he will ooze.

  Become a golfer and join his company when he invites you.

- *The Bureaucrat*: This one will demand that everything be put in writing for approval. A typical government type, who will want minutes of meetings to be properly recorded with names of who said what. All decisions, arguments, and pros and cons must be properly recorded.

  Take exhaustive notes, send the draft for approval, print it and send a copy. He wants plenty of these. The implementation of decisions, however, is another story.

- *The Leader:* You will find a very secure and centred person in him. He will try and create more leaders. He will guide, coach, and share his experiences, as well as walk the distance with you.

Make him your road model. Soak in everything he offers.

This is as far the work settings are concerned. Now let us take a look at the bosses in social settings:

- *The Clean Habit Boss:* He is not a social bird. Social settings are a waste of time. He does not approve of those who are delaying the process of dinner because they are enjoying their drinks. Lace your hard drink with a soft drink, if you are the drinking type, and if not, order a plain soda.
- *The Drinking Type*: A little-known fact of the corporate world is that it is the highest contributor to excise collection on alcohol, simply because it indulges in high-value drinking. You might land up with a boss who is a tipster and is in no hurry to eat or go home. He will repeat his stories, his jokes, and most of them will be bawdy. In such cases, do enjoy your drink, if you like, but stay sober. Do not try to compete with him, although he will egg you to. Cheat a bit because soon you may have to perform a Boy Scout role and escort your boss home, since he will be in no shape to drive. Remember that he will insist that he is fine but he is not.
- *The Leader:* Observe his appropriateness. He will be moderate in whatever he does. A fine example for you to follow.

These are the major categories of bosses you will meet, at work and socially. Follow religiously the guidelines I have given and you will be rewarded by many promotions.

Soon, you will have your own subordinates to boss/ lead over, in your very own way.

Being an
Enlightened 31
Manager

B EING THERE and not being there, are *not* opposites. They are not two poles or two extremes. They mean the same thing. You are sometimes there. You are sometimes not. When you understand how this can happen, salvation is yours. It is the ultimate managerial enlightenment. Knowing and understanding are two different things. You understand with your mind, which is a subjective exercise, depending on your biases and prejudices. On the other hand, your core being helps you to *know* at another level. Confusing? The teachings of the Buddha often confuse people initially, as do all the Zen Masters.

For true managerial bliss, you have to understand how being there and not being there mean the same thing. Bliss is an internal feeling, at the *being* level. To experience it, you don't have to learn anything new but you have to drop some past learning.

When your boss is in a guerrilla warfare mood, for example, not being there is a good policy. However, when he is tipsy and incoherent, being there to help is the best thing to do. Got it? Both are the same. Both lead to managerial bliss. Both are forms of ultimate surrender to the boss. When you surrender, there is no resistance. When there is no resistance, there is no pain and the absence of pain is bliss. That, in a nutshell, is the distilled wisdom of the Buddha's teachings to all managers, in fact, perhaps, to all humanity!

When the boss is in a sticky situation with a customer who wants to enforce a warranty clause, being there is essential to lure the customer to your office to diffuse the situation. If the matter is handled with Buddha-like awareness, we dissolve what arises. Otherwise, we resolve it only to find that the problem arises repeatedly.

When the boss is making a deal with a supplier, not being there is the right thing to do. Ignorance is bliss. When it is time to sign bills and pay tips to the waiters, so that all the expenses are accounted for in your name, being there means promotions for you. However, if after dinner, he is acting restless and pacing up and down the hotel lobby, it is likely that his out-of-town bed-mate for the night is late in arriving— don't be there! (in case you may not be sufficiently aware of why he is impatiently pacing the lobby, and want to be there, don't give in to the temptation—just quietly disappear; he knows what he is doing—you don't).

When the boss is lavishly entertaining his non-business friends and family in Mumbai, don't be there, but when he hints that the bills are adjusted in a dealers' meet expenses, make sure to be there.

When the boss's wife, and/or family, want to travel on your accumulated frequent flier travel miles, be there. However, when they are painting the town red, or shopping recklessly, don't be there. Stay there just long enough to reassure the shopkeepers that the company will honour the enormous bills raised.

Make sure you are there to become a nominal nominee director of the plethora of companies created by the boss to divert company profits, but definitely do not be there to see how these diverted funds are deployed. See no evil, hear no evil, do no evil!

Whatever gave you that idea?! Sheer escapism, or running away from the situation is not what I meant! By *being* there, you are all-knowing. Not being there also means you are still there not as a physical being but as a spiritual being, admittedly in a detached sort of manner, absorbing the goings-on around you, in a Buddha-like state. Until you are enlightened to this behaviour, the path leading to Buddha-hood can be confusing. It appears full of contradictions and paradoxes. So, not being there is not the opposite of being there but the *absence* of being there, just as darkness is not the opposite of light but rather, the absence of light. You have to learn to be invisible when the situation calls for it!

When one of your boss's golfing friends calls up and cancels the Saturday afternoon foursome, be there to fill the vacancy, otherwise don't be anywhere near the vicinity of the golf course. It is against Buddha's teaching to make your boss feel guilty. Buddha believes in experiential learning by the person himself, or herself, and not induced learning from others.

When the boss looks confused, to help dissolve his confusion, be there, but when he has that determined look on his face, don't be there. When he wants to talk about his ungrateful and unappreciative family, be there to share his burden. But when he is singing their praises, smile. Allow him to savour his short-lived happiness without sharing any of it with you.

When you are going abroad, be there to ask what you can carry for his family and friends. But when he is travelling, don't be there because he may ask you the same question!

You may be mentally questioning me at this point, that will what is being said here, make you the boss's doormat? There is no doubt that these misgivings are arising from your ego state. While there is ego, there is pain. While there is pain, there is the absence of bliss. Therefore, when you drop your ego, you reach a higher state.

'But why doesn't any book on management say that?' I hear you ask.

The management books are directed at your mind. In this case I refer more to an invisible state of being—knowing when to retreat into such a state is crucial.

'Do you mean that I should let my boss manipulate me?' you question.

Such thinking comes from the unconscious state, the ego state, or the judgemental state. We are not here to judge either our bosses or ourselves. Notice how beautifully the flowers and trees flourish. They accept nature as it is. Nature is their boss. They don't argue with nature. They are just there, and when their work is done, they are not.

'When will I know that I am an enlightened manager?' you ask.

When you stop asking questions. You were always enlightened but you have reconditioned your mind. You are always lost in thought. Drop all that conditioning, and the questions will cease. You will regain your true enlightened state. Stop searching for it because it is within you.

If you follow the path of being there and not being there, there will be bonuses. There will be rewards. There will be trips abroad. And there will be promotions. In short, there will be a state of managerial bliss. Peace and harmony will follow!

Wake Up to Your Destiny 32

IF YOU are a believer, you surely believe in destiny. If you are a non-believer, some fire is burning for you anyway. This chapter is only for believers.

You are destined to have and do many things in your life; to your spouses, your relatives, and in your work life, to the bosses you have.

If you are a fatalist, you will attain *Nirvana* (including the corporate variety) anyway, through the natural and unassisted process of evolvement. However, remember that it might take a tad too long.

If you own *responsibility* to yourself and you think of yourself as a co-creator, you can certainly hasten the process by a couple of aeons.

Stephen Covey describes responsibility as comprising two words: response and ability. Thus, responsibility means our ability to respond. He then says that you and I have no choice in what our bosses will be like. Or, for that matter what our spouses will turn out to be like, but we certainly have choices in how we will respond to these two creatures, or the situations they create for us.

Covey then advises us to create a gap between response and ability. In that gap, you have the freedom to fill your choices. *Shall I be mean to the boss, or shall I be compassionate to him? Shall I hinder or shall I help? Shall I hinder sometime or help sometime to confuse him? Shall I work for my ultimate goal or shall I work for some ethereal and abstract goals?* Being practical business people, you will choose the former and leave the second to my breed (consultants). The next step is to decide what you will fill in that gap.

At the first level of your evolvement, you will fill that gap by engaging your boss in sharing his or her expectations with you. Here, exchange refers to one-way traffic. Let him or her tell you what their expectations are. Write them down, have them vetted by the boss, clarify them, be crystal clear so that there is no ambiguity, and then carry them out to the exclusion of all else.

Remember that these expectations will keep changing. Change-ability is in the nature of dynamic bosses, as is impulsiveness. Keep their expectations under constant review.

Try not to be too smart and start putting on the table your expectations of the boss. It is not the done thing to attain corporate nirvana.

You might negotiate some expectations with him. For example, he might ask you to do some insignificant task as many will do; you could then negotiate and say, ' I will send Fix-it to you and he will do as you say in this area'. That is normal and about the only choice you have.

The second level of evolvement is accepting the boss as he/she is. Here the only choice is one of total surrender. Meditate in your office every morning to be aligned to your mission. Breathe deeply and say, 'I surrender to your will totally and unconditionally. I will do what you tell me, any minute of the day. I will not let my ego state come between your wishes and me. Your wish is my command. I am nothing. You are everything and in that lies my peace, happiness and ultimate bliss'. How many times should you repeat the mantra? Until you know that at the 'being' level, you feel aligned. You will observe that with daily practice, you will feel aligned halfway through your first chant itself.

The third level of evolvement is when you drop all expectations, not only from your boss but also of yourself. Being fatalistic? No. Out of this approach comes a new spiritual power to face any challenges, any obstacles, any disappointments. When you reach this level, you can even face with equanimity, one of your colleagues getting a promotion for your hard work. You don't flip into a depression on a minor nuisance of being passed over. You have thus nearly arrived at your destination on the path of corporate nirvana.

In the final stage of evolvement, you ask yourself an all-powerful question: *What does love for my boss require me to do now?* Every time you are faced with a situation created by the boss, ask yourself this question. Out of loving questions will come loving solutions, free of hate, disunity, and fragmentation. The solutions will be whole and complete and you will find that Nature will not resist them because they come out of your loving nature. You will feel fulfilled.

As a consultant and a counsellor, I see many fractured managerial souls and find that there is little teaching done on the subject.

What is the reason for this malady? The main reason is that the B-schools continue to pursue academic excellence, exploiting your high level of intelligence.

But spirituality is missing and spirituality is the foundation of all living and coping. Therefore, working managers create for themselves one of the following three psychological conditions and ruin their bright careers: they become co-dependent, over-dependent, or counter-dependent on their bosses. They continue to operate in the realm of the mind.

Co-dependency is like addiction to alcohol or substance abuse. This category can't do without their boss. They need him/her even to change their managerial nappies. They reach for their boss, as an addict reaches for the bottle first thing in the morning. They keep their hand near the telephone hoping that the boss will call and they will get to have a sip of distilled wisdom from them. They cannot operate without his guidance.

Over-dependence is a different kind of psychological condition. In this case, managers leave everyone else out of the reckoning. The boss and only the boss is on their radarscope. They fail because eventually all work has to be done in teams and the teams feel switched off. No good again.

The third condition is exactly the opposite of over-dependence and, therefore, more deadly than the first two. In this condition, managers are hostile towards their bosses and thereby lose their trust. Managers suffering from this condition are generally popular with their colleagues and subordinates.

These conditions lead managers to hold unrealistic views of what a boss is. That is their downfall. That is the root of their managerial suffering.

Part V

On
Business
Etiquette

A Small Matter of Packaging Ourselves
33

W HEN WE returned from the Lake District to London, with good old Bill at the wheel, me strapped by his side and our wives comfortably stretched in the rear, I couldn't help noticing Bill's loud printed red shirt.

So, I couldn't help remarking: 'Bill, this shirt is too much! Mary, I hope all is well with Bill's world and head?' Mary was quick to put the blame squarely on me for this sudden change in Bill's selection of colour. She said, 'Remember, Dinesh, you said something like us English not knowing any colour beyond the dull greys and browns. So Bill thought he would shock you with this blood-red printed shirt.'

That was sufficient for Bill to launch another tirade on all the Indians imprisoned in his car.

'Mary, at least I am wearing this shirt on holiday, unlike some of my Indian friends here who wear such loud clothes at the workplace as if it was just the matter of putting on the first shirt that's hanging in their cupboards.'

'Is that why you wear dark glasses even inside a room there?' Mary egged him on.

I knew that I had put my foot in the wrong place by taking a shot at the dull and drab English outfits because there was no stopping his invective. Bill is articulate, if nothing else.

'Dinesh, let me tell you a thing or two. We dress to enhance our personality and not distract from it like Indians dress, as if it were an exercise to show off your wardrobe. It is one thing to have a riot of colour, it is yet another to use the colours appropriately. Dress sense, my dear man, it is all about dress sense', said good old Bill pompously.

'What about it?' is all I had to say, to hear a thesis on work clothes.

'First, don't punish me again like you did the last time, packing me off to Mysore with one of your VPs who was wearing a nylon shirt. I was about to puke in the car because the fellow's synthetic shirt stank.'

'OK, OK, don't make such big deal out of it,' I protested.

'I will. It is a big deal as far as I am concerned. An air-conditioned room or car and nylon clothes is a deadly combination as far as the foul smell index is concerned. I remember it was a wet, muggy afternoon in July. I felt I was locked up in a toilet for three hours. Just the thought of it makes me sick!'

I tried to change the subject when my wife intervened.

'Don't you dare change the subject! Bill, carry on, I have a thing or two to say on this issue myself.'

'I think you should ban anything other than cottons in the climatic conditions that you have there, and I am sure you chaps have heard of something called a deodorant? I am sure that they must be available in India by now?' Bill is at his best when he is sarcastic.

Mary said that Bill liked to dress appropriately. He would return home after the meetings with Indian companies and then regale her with the stories such as the one of a manager who had such long nails that Harry could not concentrate what the fellow was saying. Or about another who knotted a tie so badly that it did not even reach his belt.

Clothes are a subject of great interest to my dear wife and, therefore, this time, instead of sleeping in a moving car as is her wont, she stayed glued to every word.

'Do tell your friend, Bill, to go for value-for-money clothes. He buys cheap suits that shrink on him. I also think that the dark-skinned people should choose relatively lighter shades', added my wife.

She found perfect allies in Bill and Mary when she said that she wanted to throw away all the clothes I owned which have fraying collars and cuffs because for her wearing frayed clothes simply makes a bad statement of one's personality.

What Bill was saying appealed to me because I also believe that at the workplace, one should be appropriately dressed. No T-shirts, for me at least. Golf ties are fine for the golf club but I am not sure that they belong to the workplace.

I remembered how often I felt like sending the guys in loafers back home to change into nicely polished shoes. Next time, I will probably do that.

My wife did not want to miss any opportunity to square up with me and said, 'I keep telling Dinesh that he has to select his socks to match the clothes he wears. It's not as simple as wearing any pair of socks with any pair of shoes or clothes, but does he listen?'

I took out my little pad and asked Bill if he had any other pearls of wisdom for me to carry home. He asked me whether I planned to do a PowerPoint presentation back home. I said maybe.

'How many times do we have to be told that right clothes give an executive a sense of poise and confidence?' he added.

'Agreed,' I said.

'I truly believe that a slovenly-dressed man gives himself up as a disorganized man,' he said with passion.

'And those cowboy-sized belt buckles. Ugh.'

I nodded in agreement. It was now the turn of the lady of the house to make her remarks.

'It does not take a large wardrobe to look elegant. Four well-coordinated outfits are any day better than the thoughtless purchases you make at Marks and Spencer. You know Bill, I don't let him buy any clothes. I select them for him.'

I squirmed.

'For Pete's sake, shave everyday and if you choose to keep a beard, then trim it regularly and keep it neat.' Bill interjected.

'What else, Bill? Tell me the whole story and be done with it.'

'I will if you will take back that remark about us English being such bores in the matter of dressing,' he demanded.

'Nothing ever will make me change my mind on that one. You are grey and colourless and that is that.' I held my ground.

'So, tell them that they should take care of packaging themselves as much as they do for the products.' He fumed.

'While I am at it, ladies, do you have anything to add for yourselves?' I asked.

'We ladies have much more common sense than the species sitting in the front seats,' my wife remarked.

'I am giving you a chance to share your wisdom on the subject. Maybe I am assuming too much,' I said to prod them.

For ladies, this is what they advised:

- The use of provocative clothes at the workplace is a strict no-no situation.
- Wear light perfume. Your perfume should follow you rather than precede you.

- Use subdued nail polish.
- Carry a handbag that is not so unwieldy that it needs a table in its own right.

I told them that it was not much by way of advice. Women, they believed, knew where to draw the line.

Bill and I looked at each other and knew that the last word had been said on this topic. So, Bill picked his favourite subject and that was Tony Blair.

Eating with Implements 34

D ID YOU know that those things we call knives, forks and spoons, are known as dining implements? Frankly, I did not. I discovered this when we were having our pre-departure dinner with Bill and Mary.

These dinners were jocularly referred to as 'Getting Rid of the Kumars'. They were always arranged in proper British settings. Despite all the training the defence services had given me in dining etiquette, occasions like formal dinners sometimes overwhelm me. The nagging question always is, *am I doing the right thing?*

The lady of the house has no such problem. Her theory is simple. Observe others and follow their example when you are not sure of what to do. Or ask a question.

Restaurant situations always warm her up, and as we settled down she struck this note.

'Bill, back home Dinesh keeps complaining that the managers in his company are very uncomfortable when they are eating out with guests. Particularly when guests from other countries are visiting, because they are not sure what is appropriate and what is not in formal settings.'

'I see no point in bringing domestic complaints under the purview of British adjudication', I retorted, finding that the subject was a bit of a sore point between us.

Her point was that if lack of comfort were the issue, it wouldn't disappear by wishing it away.

'Either you stop complaining or do something about it.' It was clear that the English couple and my wife were quite enjoying my discomfort.

My friend Bill does not need more than half a chance to teach Indians etiquette, as I have demonstrated previously.

'Frankly, I agree with Jaya, that if there is an inadequacy in the system, it must be addressed. It will not just go away. I don't know whether it would help if I tell you that when the Japs were entering the global business scene, the first thing they did was to teach their people the culture of the country and the Western mores of entertaining.'

'You mean they took classes in etiquette?' I asked.

'They jolly well did exactly that. They even held practical classes, took their chaps out for dinner, and gave them tips as the meal proceeded.'

'Really?' I was incredulous.

'No, Dinesh, I am just making it up,' Bill responded. That shut me up right and proper.

Bill proceeded to say, 'Frankly, I have observed some of these things when I visit Indian companies but always thought, who am I? It is an Indian problem. Let them handle it. But if you ever get down to doing something, start with the belch bursting.' Mary frowned at Bill for this unsolicited advice.

'What else have you noticed, Bill?' I asked.

'There is nothing like a free dinner. If you promise to pick up the tab for the cognac, which I plan to have by the fireside in the anteroom of the restaurant, we can shake hands on that.' Bill wanted his pound of flesh and I was willing to pay.

'How frank can I be?' he asked.

'As frank as possible.' I assured him.

'Dinesh, the last time I was there, your vice-president arrived with his colleagues a good 15 minutes after we had reached the restaurant. I had half a mind to return to the hotel but Mary stopped me. Awful way to start an evening. Moreover, the chief host grandly sat down while Mary was still struggling with her seat. Not done. 'And then your chaps started looking at the menu, while Mary had this look on her face which said, *these chaps must be really hungry.*'

'You mean they should have let you order first?' I asked.

'Not only that, they should help you with the selection of something special that the place may be known for and then take our order and pass it to the steward.' Bill emphasised.

'Come on Bill, you don't expect your host to take out a pen and paper and write down your order. I mean this is carrying things too far', I protested.

'Not expected when the group is large, but certainly if you have three or four guests. It is also very annoying that when this ordering process is going on, you start talking some business or any other matter.' Bill said.

'Bill, I like having wine but don't know which wine to order with what food. So I stick to whisky and soda', I added.

'I have been telling you that it is not just about which wine is served with what food any more. It was important before, not any longer.' My convent-educated wife interrupted.

'That is true. Things are a lot less formal than they used to be. Having said that, the importance of good table manners cannot be relegated when hosting business lunches or dinners.'

'Like what', I asked, prompting Bill.

'Like always extending invitations yourselves. Like arriving on time. Like giving the best view seats to the guests. Like doing a bit of planning. I always liken the job of the host to an orchestra conductor, who must harmonise the dinner.'

'One thing that upsets me when Dinesh calls his colleagues home, is that they break into business talk and we ladies find it very boring', my wife remarked.

'Not done', Bill said, looking at me like a stern school teacher. 'In any case, in a restaurant setting, even when one is only with business guests, business talk should be kept to the minimum and then too after all the orders have been placed and the waiters are out of the way', he continued.

'Supposing I were to take the Japanese approach in our company, what ought I to be doing?' I asked because I knew sooner or later the issue would have to be tackled.

'If I were doing it, I would explain very gently the need for some formal education. Just knowing a few things can help us to enjoy our meal. I will give you just one example. If you accidentally knock off something you can fuss the whole evening and spoil it but if you knew better, you can apologise and move and let the waiter take care of the damage,' Bill said.

That was making a lot of sense.

'I hope you won't get me wrong when I say that your chaps have a habit of filling the plate in one go. It is so much better if one takes food in manageable portions. Or eating and talking simultaneously.'

'Go on, I am with you', I said, not wishing to miss out on anything important.

'There is no point pushing hard liquor on people who choose to abstain on a day for their own reason.'

'Sometimes, with all our planning, I find the best of the establishments make a mess of the whole thing by poor standard of food or service,' I said, sharing my experience.

'True, but often we make the situation worse by hauling up the steward and making a scene. Register our displeasure, we must. After all, we are paying for the service and we want good service but only after the guests have left.'

After a moment, he added, 'It is never appropriate for the guests to complain about the quality of food or service. If they do that, indirectly they are reflecting on the choice of their hosts.'

'Anything else, now that we are about to finish the meal?', I asked.

'Looking at your watches indicates, "when will this ordeal be over?". Finishing your meal too quickly, as if you had a train to catch, or making a big issue of checking and double checking your bill and fussing over some mistake. All that can be done after the guests have left.'

'The funny thing is that we are about to finish our dinner and we didn't even get talking about the dining implements.' I said.

'I think I'll let your wife give you lessons on that one!' said Bill, ending our discussion on driving etiquette.

I grunted in response as we moved to the ante-room for some cognac by the fireside.

Conversationally Yours   35

B ILL AND Mary, a charming English couple, have become more than just our business friends. We take holidays together, the last of which was in the Lake Districts in the UK.

Bill generally drives, while I do the map reading for him. Mary participates and my wife doses off and starts snoring before the car is in the fourth gear.

Bill and I like provoking each other to get the conversation going. The verbal bouts between us may have something to do with our common history.

This is what happened on this journey.

I said, 'Your friend Tony is no more than an Assistant Foreign Secretary of the US, going by the way he toes the American policies.' Instead of being provoked, he blandly replied, 'I totally agree. And he is no friend of mine.' I had forgotten that Bill was a confirmed Tory.

I tried another tack and said, 'Bill, you British must be the most boring people on the face of this planet.'

'Why would you say that?' demanded Bill.

'You are the only people I know, who can travel on the same train day after day, sit next to each other, absorbed in your newspapers, and not even know your neighbour's name!'

That was sufficient fuel to fire a full-blooded tirade.

'That is better than your countrymen! Yours must be the only country where everyone talks to every-one else without even knowing the other, mostly simultaneously and still understands the other!' Bill said passionately.

'Come, come Bill. I thought you English spoke in understatements. This is a gross exaggeration', I replied with matching intensity.

'Your conferences are chaotic. Everyone is chipping in his opinion. No one waits for his turn and people indulge in loud conversation from one end of the table to the other without saying as much as, *excuse me.*'

'Come, on, Bill', I tried to calm him.

'If you don't believe me, next time I come for the meetings, I will record the proceedings and play them for you,' Bill replied.

I knew that I was on a weak wicket. I knew that neither companies, nor business schools, taught business etiquette to their managers, and very often, senior people were in breach of manners in many business and social settings.

I said, lamely, 'You are right. We could do with some polish in this area.'

'Polish? What you need is a good scrub', piped in Mary, and added, 'Last time, I was very embarrassed when a total stranger in a party walked up to me, extended his hand to shake mine and introduced himself.'

'You should have taught us all this when you were ruling us for centuries', I said to him half jokingly.

'One more blame on us, and you got rid of us over 50 years ago', said Bill. 'A man should never offer to shake a lady's hand. It is only a woman's privilege to take that initiative.'

My wife woke up and said that exactly the same thing often happens to her, and therefore, just to be polite, she takes the hand if any man extends it. She said she was not sure of what was the right thing to do.

'You do the right thing, girl', said Bill. 'If a man extends his hand, a lady should accept it. I don't know who said that a firm handshake gives a first good impression and you will never be forgiven if you don't live up to it.'

'Take it down then,' I volunteered. 'It was P.J. Rourke in *Modern Manners*'. And then, just to rub it in, I said, 'Bill, it is a good habit to give your source when you quote someone.'

'There is another thing that you fellows do that I find irksome. You will introduce me to someone, vanish, and leave us in an embarrassing silence. Why don't you tell us something that interests us both, so that we have a basis for conversation?' Bill continued.

'Like what?' asked my wife.

'Oh, a good concert or a play, or books, or whatever,' Bill explained.

That made sense because often I was stuck with a total stranger without knowing how to break the proverbial ice.

Bill was warming up. He winked at his wife and said, 'Mary, shall we give our Indian friends some lessons in the art of conversation?'

'Well if they promise to pick up the tab at the pub this evening, I see no harm', Mary replied.

'Okay then, here we go. Remember a junior is introduced to a senior, a gent to a lady, a single woman to a married woman', continued Bill. 'There is only one exception though. Everyone is introduced to a celebrity. I would be a nut to say: Mr Prime Minister, please meet my wife, Mary. Mary is a retired school teacher and takes her profession very seriously, even at home.'

It was clear that Mary was not amused with the example.

'Now Bill, you are saying the obvious', I said.

'Obvious to you and me, Dinesh because you and I were told this when we were in the defence forces.' said Bill.

'This handshake stuff, Bill, some handshakes are so limp and sweaty that you don't know whether you are dealing with a man or a wimp', I said.

'I could live with that variety. It is the bone-crushing machos that bother me,' added Mary.

'We have drifted a bit haven't we, love?' Bill said, 'We started with cross talk and ended up with handshakes.'

'I plead guilty to that. I was the one who brought up the handshake business,' I said.

I was not sure whether I had done the right thing by earlier making that statement about the staid and ever-so-private British but Bill was making a lot of sense.

'There is another thing that irritates me when I come to India. You have so many languages and everyone breaks into his or her own language', Bill fumed.

Since I had been a victim of this transgression, I said, 'Don't worry Bill, when I go back I will declare to my people in the Mark Antony style: 'Friends, Indians and countrymen, Bill is not a bad chap. He loves Indian food. He just does not understand our language. Please speak in the language that he and all others around you understand.'

'While you are at it, you might even tell them not to speak to one another in whispers. By the way, old chap, I hope I am not offending you. Let me admit that talking in whispers is almost a universal malady. Even we too sometimes indulge in it.'

I did not miss observing the emphasis on *sometimes*. Mary reminded Bill that if he carried on like this, he would lose us as friends.

'Talking about manners, Bill, have you noticed how you have hogged the whole conversation? I won't say that this is the best example of polite conversation. You were so busy that you completely forgot to take the exit into Hawkstead.

Bill had set a chain of thoughts in me. So often we use slang, tell off-colour jokes, argue loudly, gossip, scandalise people, rip personalities and use expletives, all in the name of modernity. The worst example that came to my mind was poking fun at those with a disability, a lisp, or something else over which they had no control.

Bill asked me what I was thinking and when I told him, he responded, 'That is patently bad.'

At this stage Bill spotted a 100-year old pub and said, 'Dear, shall we collect our fee from our Indian friend before we check in at the hotel?'

I was ready to pay up because I too was thirsty. My wife got up when the car stopped and asked, 'Have we reached?'

I jumped out of the car and opened the car door for Mary, while Bill did the same for my wife.

'See Mary, our lessons are already taking effect,' Bill declared triumphantly.

Scott M. Peck, my spiritual guru, says that if someone sheds light on your ignorance, embrace him. Bill is a bit too big for one embrace.

I Just Called to Say 'I Love You' 36

A TELEPHONE call can be terribly intrusive at the wrong time, even if it is from a close friend. It can ruin your mood and put an end to the peaceful day you were having.

I remember a day like that—shot to hell because of a telephone. It was from my computer guy, who, after breaking three appointments, finally turned up at my office an hour late. I get murderous thoughts when people arrive late for appointments, and to top it all, this man entered my office, with his cell phone stuck to his right ear, deep in conversation with one of his clients.

During the couple of hours that he spent with me, he must have spent around 30 minutes (of my time) talking to his clients (mostly explaining why he had not turned up to see them at the appointed time). His audacious behaviour included billing me for the time! Us old economy folks can really be taken for a ride! I'd like to think that we are much more honest. Comparatively speaking, that is.

He was lucky that I noticed the hacksaw in the garage only after he had left my office.

I had barely settled back to work when there was a knock on the door. My next visitor was a fellow member of a club I belong to. He said that he was passing by and had decided to drop in to say hello to me. Arriving without an appointment raised my blood pressure level—and when I saw his companion (a cell phone) it went up higher. Of course, throughout his visit, it rang incessantly and he talked nonstop without even saying *excuse me* while he took his calls. I was about to box him in the ear when my telephone rang. It was my son (on his cell phone) who told me that he was at the gate and would I open it. He had decided to drop in to have lunch with his mother and me. He obviously didn't think of getting out of the car and ringing the doorbell!

Well, lunch was pleasant. The annoying part was when he used one hand to eat and the other to hold his cell phone while he dispatched generators from his factory to customers located all over India,

I JUST CALLED TO SAY 'I LOVE YOU'

making sweeping gestures now and then with rice-covered fingers. And when he ordered a dispatch north to Guwahati, he knocked my hot *rassam* all over my shirt.

We used to have much better table manners at their age in our time, didn't we?

To complete my miserable Saturday, we were doing some compulsory entertaining. 'Compulsory' because we were returning hospitality received some aeons ago. Delayed any further, there was a real danger of being struck off from our guests' list of invitees.

Unlike my industry friends, as a mere consultant, I have to double up as the bartender. So with two drinks in either hand all I was doing was chasing two busy bees walking up and down the lawn talking on their cell phones. I wanted to pour the whisky over their heads. Four such cell-phone invasions in one day are a bit much. Don't you think so?

Over dinner, our guests were not telling jokes like we used to but were passing them around on their cell phones. 'Read this', one would say and it did not take long for the other to say, 'Have you seen this one?' (The only compensation here was that there were some very raunchy jokes, which I thoroughly enjoy!)

When the guests had left, I poured myself a stiff shot of XO cognac, to return to some sanity (and help me sleep). It put me into a contemplative mood and I was transported to the times when I was a young officer in the Indian Airforce. We were taught etiquette with the help of a book, titled *Etiquette of Service*. With great difficulty I tried to recall some of the tips on phone etiquette that I had forgotten, most of them through disuse.

One of the things I clearly remembered was that a telephone call is perceived as an intrusion in your schedule and to return it only at a convenient time.

The book also told us that it was polite to ask the person you had called whether it was OK to continue the conversation, or would some other time be convenient. Another was that when you meet people and the meeting might result in having to make calls to one another, it is a good time to establish what would be a convenient time to call the other person.

Now I convert my telephone conversations into a bit of fun. When I hear a lovely voice saying 'Who is speaking?' I want to say, 'Your friend', but can't take a chance, not knowing who it is on the other end! It could be a rusty old person who might take me seriously. And then what?!

Some people, after asking who I am, assume that I will recognise their voice and don't tell me their names. I am supposed to do some guesswork here. So, just to poke fun at them, after they have finished saying what they have to say, I ask, 'who is speaking?' (I do this even if I know who it is on the other line). When they tell me their name, I say for good measure, 'I thought so! Who else could it be but you!'

The most annoying are the people who call and say 'wrong number' with no apologies for doing so. When I have the time, I tell them caustically, 'I am *so* sorry to have caused you so much inconvenience'. Although I think I'm being helpful, a World War I vintage friend tells me that I am being sarcastic. So if someone asks, 'Who is this?' I reply 'Whom do you want?' To 'What number is this?' I reply 'What number do you want?'

I once got a lucrative assignment because the big boss forgot some ordinary telephone etiquette. While I was with him, he kept answering calls on the speaker phone. During one of these calls the person on the other line said, 'You know, sir, this guy sitting in front of you is a big hoax. He does not know a sausage about management. I met him in my previous company and he only wasted our time.' The boss was so embarrassed that he hired me—and the sneaking vice-president became my student yet again.

I am sure I've got a chronic case of telephone trauma! I think it's time I founded a telephone terror club (or should it be terrorised club?). I will be the president. The vacancy for a pretty secretary is wide open.

C
O
R
P
O
R
A
T
E

C
A
P
E
R
S

Part VI

On
Second
Thoughts

Blowing up
Management   37
Myths

THERE ARE many management myths that, at face value, sound quite logical. Thus, we naturally begin to believe that if we don't follow them, we are messing up things. So these myths continue to persist for generations. The breeding ground of these stories are companies whose overriding philosophy is that *we have always done it this way, haven't we?*

Myth # 1: The Management and the Union have Adversarial Aims

This comes from the belief that all workers are shirkers. That if they realise the true state of affairs, there will be no end to their demands. They will exploit any chink that they see in the management's armour. Therefore, keep them at arm's length, as far as management issues are concerned. By doing this, the management has already created an adversary in their minds and it soon begins to reflect in all their actions. Any request, however, reasonable it might be, is rejected out of hand.

I once worked for a company, where the finance director was our chief wage negotiator with the labour union. He would start his opening bid during wage negotiations with Rs 50. It would matter little to him that in an earlier settlement conducted only three or four years previously, the amount given was Rs 350. Of course, the opening bid of the union was never less than Rs 1500. After one year of negotiations, tool-down strikes, and sometimes, even lockouts, we would settle for Rs 500.

The worst part was that this chief negotiator would then strut like a peacock and claim victory that he upped his bid only by Rs 450 but the climb down by the union was Rs 1000! It never occurred to him, that the workers, over whom he thought he'd scored a victory, were the same people that he had selected. They were also a part of the same organic set up of which he was a part.

This utterly foolish practice carried on for many years, till we started behaving like adults and of course we got an adult response from the union. Believe me, managements tell *white* lies while dealing with their unions. They give the wrong information about the company's profits while negotiating the wages. They fail to remember that the finance clerk, who types the real figures, is a union member. The union leaders know exactly what those figures are. By this one act, unions rightly come to a conclusion that whatever be the designations of people they are dealing with, they are no more than bunch of manipulating liars.

So, the workers have no choice but to take an agitational approach, even if the struggle requires feeding an expensive, political labour leader. In any event, the management deserves the union they get.

Myth # 2: Customers Want the Best at the Cheapest Prices

This is true of perhaps 5 per cent of customers. It amazes me that 95 per cent of companies tailor their policies and attitude based on the experience they have with this 5 per cent. My marketing experience tells me that if you place trust on the negotiating table for the customer to see, and if he can see that trust in your eyes, the chances are greater then that even he would match trust with trust. He wants it to be a win-win situation. He needs to deal with a healthy company. He wants to play in a league of his own.

In the case of those 5 per cent, who play for lose-win, it may be wise to tell your customers that unless it is a win-win situation for both of you, you will have no truck with them. Politely, of course with your manners, intact. The best part of this approach is that you are placing such customers in the lap of the competition. Let the competition handle the selfish ones.

Data shows that customers leave you for the competition reluctantly, only when they have been treated unfairly and even after many complaints, you continue to behave in an unethical and non- responsive manner.

Whenever I see a sign in a shop, which says 'goods once sold cannot be exchanged or returned', I make it a point to ask them a patent question, 'How many customers come back for replacements or refunds?' The answer invariably is 'very few'. I look at the sign, make my point and walk out. And never miss to see a sheepish smile on their faces but the sign stays.

Some of my best friends are my former customers. They were honourable buyers. Many times, we had to say *no* to each other for our internal compulsions but that only consolidated the equation of mutual respect and trust.

Myth # 3: Multiple Suppliers Mean Better Quality Products at Better Prices

This is a myth, which is very difficult to explode because it is so logical. You have got to play one against the other to get the best, they tell me. But wait till you have heard me out.

If you have five suppliers for a product that you need and none of them is sure whether he will be on your list of suppliers next year, what do you think is their motivation level to invest in improvements? Also, remember that they are getting only 20 per cent of your total business and, therefore, there is not enough volume of work to obtain a cost advantage. Most importantly, production guys hate multiple suppliers. They know two basic truths. First, that multiple suppliers mean variation in the quality standard and the second, that variation in quality is their biggest enemy. They know it is going to be a back-breaking job to sit down and rework the variable qualities of different suppliers to fit their requirement.

You may think that if it is as obvious as that, do you think that the companies are so blind that they can't see the advantages? Precisely, since they are not exactly blind but they are definitely myopic. They see the obvious up-front costs. They miss out the cost the companies pay for reworking and rejection. Since these managers can only see the visible numbers, the invisible cost of frustration, low morale and delays does not figure in their calculation.

Look at it another way. You have an ongoing arrangement with one or two suppliers who know that their future is tied up with you and that working with you is in their mutual interest. It also means that they will be getting bulk orders. What are they likely to do? Give you bulk discounts and invest in plant and machinery.

As purchasers, it is your direct responsibility to work with your suppliers to help them improve quality. Now, ask yourself whether you really have the resources to provide assistance to a large number of them.

Do keep in mind that this myth is the hardest to break. When I am discussing this concept with a group of managers, I can easily spot those who have cynical smiles appearing on their faces. Sooner and later, they will get up and say that if they follow this policy, the suppliers will take them for a ride. Now, I know that I am looking at managers who, as far as I am concerned, are making an open declaration that it is quite easy to take them for a ride. They forget that no one can take you for a ride without your permission. There is an assumption here that you will choose your partners wisely.

When nothing else works, I ask the marketing managers sitting there what they would rather choose. Would they prefer to have a small percentage of their customer's business or would they rather have all of it? The answer, invariably, is that they would like 100 per cent of their customers' business. The reason they give me, is that with 100 per cent business, they will be able to do the best for their customers in prices and quality standards. Do you see the double standards? We want to have 100 per cent of others' businesses but we are not willing to give the same treatment to our suppliers. Sometimes, even this argument does not work and I give up considering the cost of making my case is more than convincing a few selfish people.

Myth # 4: Leaders Must Always Lead from the Front

If you are sitting at the edge of your seat reading this chapter, I don't blame you. Leaders must lead and the word 'lead' means that they must be up-front. Leaders lead, followers follow. Right? Not always. In my view, it is a leader's job to create the context of working in an organisation. That is his most important function. He is eminently positioned to create that context because his office is situated on the top floor. But he can cause that context to happen without always being in the front rank.

In my view, successful leaders in the future will not be talking in terms of 'span of control'. They will talk about the span of support. Their language will be something like 'I support the effort of 4000 people in this organisation'. They will abhor the term 'span of control'. I see future leaders as spiritual leaders, who know that there are many fractured and hurt souls in their companies. They know that these people perform below their potential because they are dealing with issues that they cannot cope with. They will set about healing these poor souls and the returns they will get from their people will be beyond measure. Some would say that the soft approach does not work. Soft is often hard to practice in management and, therefore, is left to a few brave leaders.

So, leaders are required to create a context of working. What kind of context do we expect good leaders to create? *A context in which everyone in the company regards the other as his customer*. It must be remembered that others receive the result of the efforts we make in an organisation. The question is whether we can consider that department or that person as our esteemed customers.

For instance, if a leader can make the purchase department consider the production department as its most esteemed customer, and if he can do the same with the production department, then, for them, the very rationale of their existence is to delight the marketing department. And so on in the chain of work in a company.

I refer to leaders who are not necessarily the most visible people in the organisation. But they create a context of work in which people know that whenever there is an obstruction to their work like inadequate training, or insufficient funds, they can walk into the leader's office and be sure that it will be taken care of.

They know that if they fail or fall in their effort, their leader will be their safety net. The leader will allow you to fall, but only forward. Leaders will teach you to lead from the front, while they give you all the support you need from the back. They will provide you with the space to make your own decisions. In the event of a mistake, instead of a reprimand, you will be told *I hope it has been a good experience for you and you have learnt something from it.*

Myth # 5: A Certain Amount of Fear is Necessary to Get the Best Out of Others

The trouble with this concept is that we are never sure what that 'certain' amount is. Also, most people who advocate this concept hate a 'certain' amount of fear applied to them. Fear, for them is alright when it is applied to others but not so good when it is applied to them. People persist with this myth because they have never experienced the absence of fear in their lives. They lived in fear of their parents while they were growing up; and they have lived in fear of their bosses. I have seen workers literally cling to the wall while their manager angrily marches down the middle of the corridor. Some people believe the workers do it out of respect. It is plain fear, and the manager enjoys seeing it. This sort of behaviour has nothing to do with respect.

My experience about fear says exactly the opposite. When fear is present, facts are missing. Suggestion boxes are empty. It is safer to keep your mouth shut than to open it.

In such organisations, the management denies itself a free treasure-trove of suggestions that can come from workers to improve the quality of the company's products and services. That is because the greatest fear in an organisation is the fear of ridicule. *I don't know what the boss man will say if I give this suggestion. Perhaps I know what he will say. Perhaps he will repeat what he said last time, that it was the dumbest suggestion he had ever heard in years.*

I ask the promoters of this myth how they felt working for a fear-driven organisation. It is not what they say that is important to me. It is losing eye contact with them at that stage which is a dead give-away. Of course, a certain amount of fear is important when applied to others but it is a curse when applied to you. You are OK. It is just that others are not.

The question of *a certain amount* is still unresolved. What amount is *certain* and what is not? Who decides the amount? The transmitter of fear or the receiver?

Myth # 6: Delay in Payments to your Suppliers Improves Cash Flow

You will hear managers shout from the top of the roof and declare, 'Ladies and gentlemen. Positive cash flow is the lifeline of a business. Money is the lubricant of a commercial activity. We want to be a debt-free company to improve our profitability'. After making those lofty statements, they return to their offices and you hear them tell their finance manager, 'See if you can delay the payment as long as possible.' Little do they realise that their counterpart has a similar aim of converting his company into a debt-free one. What's good for the goose is always good for the gander.

Soon, the supplier realises your intention. So, you become his last priority. He first wants to finish all the orders of the good paymasters. Then comes your turn. You start getting your supplies at the end of the month, which seriously disturbs your production cycle. Then comes that fateful day when non-supply of one part from him is holding up something that costs a fortune in terms of billing and reputation.

Now he has caught you where it hurts you the most. Then he stops receiving your calls. You are told that he is travelling, that he has gone for some urgent work, when you know that he is sitting in his office and enjoying seeing you squirm. Then suddenly, all his payments are released. Presto, the missing part appears. Your neck was in your customer's noose and your supplier received his payment as a result. If money is the lifeline of your business, think about whether the same principle applies to your suppliers. My dentist says that my teeth are not in very good shape. Naturally, I have been grinding them, seeing these double standards for such a long time.

Myth # 7: Let Workers Work. Let Managers Manage

Our cook manages the kitchen much better than my wife does. He has arranged everything in such a way that he can operate efficiently. Any other way will tire him out and make him less productive. He did not always do it that way. He learnt from experience. Whenever my wife, the manager of the house, goes to the kitchen (which mercifully, is rare), there is total chaos. She does not realise that things have changed in the 30 years since she last managed the kitchen by herself.

It is the same with managers. They are supposed to know everything and, therefore, in one sweep of a visit they alter arrangements, and make managerial decisions that really lie in the domain of workers. They, like our cook, have the right experience to manage their environment.

Always, always, consult the worker and get his agreement before you make any changes. Get his buy in; otherwise he will do exactly the same thing our cook does, which is rearrange things as soon as he sees the *memsahib* leave the kitchen.

These then are the six myths that managements have lived with for generations. I once asked an MD why the employee contract form for his managers was so long and laborious. Also, why it included so many unenforceable clauses, and whether in this day and age, it made sense to keep a person on probation on each step of promotion even if he had worked for a quarter of a century. His reply did not shock me when he said that there must be some purpose in that clause when his grandfather designed it.

Do you see the *we-have-always-done-it-that-way* mentality in his statement?

Let me close by saying that you should not take what I have discussed here for granted but put them to test and taste the experience yourself. The choices in life, remember, are always yours.

Fear is Not the Key 38

A LONG time ago, a Hollywood movie titled *Fear is the Key* became a hit. I suspect that a lot of corporate big chiefs and middle managers saw the film and imbibed fear as a key to managing people. Fear, in many organisations, has become an instrument of the command and control structure and the policy of management. Little do these chiefs realise, that the cost of fear is far greater than all the others like poor quality, wastage, absenteeism, put together.

Recently, my wife and I attended a workshop in a voluntary organisation of which we are members.

When my wife asked a question, it was brusquely brushed aside as irrelevant. The reply to another question was a counter question. It is then that I realised that fear had also become a management tool in voluntary organisations. At the end of the workshop, we were full of knowledge but also filled with anger. The treatment of questions in the way I have described is a subtle way by which fear is induced. The most commonly used 'innocent' phrase, 'this is the silliest suggestion I have heard', is another medium of fear.

Dr Deming, the quality guru who revived the shattered Japanese economy by introducing total quality management in Japanese companies, realised the devastating effect of fear. It is no wonder then that amongst his 14 points of advice to management, one of the points reads, 'drive out fear so that everyone may work effectively for the company'. I know of two companies, which went under, because nobody dared tell the owners the facts, although the signs of sickness had appeared many years before the final blow.

The first casualty of fear in an organization is truth. Managements never really know what is going on in their organisations. They only get to know what pleases them. The facts are swept under the carpet. People spend too much time worrying, instead of working, which makes them more prone to mistakes. In the voluntary organisation mentioned above, many of the policy initiatives are not working on the ground. A lot of unnecessary paper work is generated but who will bell the cat in such a fear-filled organisation?

Managements often do not realise the appalling economic loss their companies are making on account of fear, and therefore, the balance sheets don't show this loss under any head of account and the company haemorrhages. In voluntary organisations, this loss is represented in low morale and frustration.

What kind of fears are generally present in companies? The most common is the fear of ridicule; the ultimate one is the fear of losing your job. The top managements continue to argue that a 'certain' amount of fear is necessary to instill discipline. The difficulty is that soon 'certain' becomes uncertain. The impression I get out of these discussions is that 'fear is good when applied to others but not so good when applied to me'.

Here is an invitation to the readers to dwell over just one issue. If you belong to a company where the variation between performance and promise is large and this happens year after after year, you are most likely working for a fear-driven company. People are too scared to tell the management that they won't be able to deliver on the promise being drafted in the corporate office.

Why do managers follow such a destructive policy? Remember, all our actions stem from our beliefs, our guiding principles. If my belief is that people are generally lazy, dishonest, and shirkers, my policies would be based on the stick and carrot principle. It is in such organisations the word mentor is ridiculed. The term supervisor is more appropriate and prevalent except that the vision of the supervisors is not all that super. It is my hypothesis that those Indian companies, which are fear-driven, will never be globally competitive. On this hypothesis, I am willing to put my neck on line.

You can sense the health of the company you are visiting in the first one hour. One sure shot indicator is how much fun people are having while working together. The way you are greeted and escorted will tell you more about the company than all the mission statements hung on the wall.

Let me end this chapter with an anecdote. The export director of a company in France was taking me around the shop floor. At the end of the walk around, we went back to the office of the managing director. The export director told me that I could ask the 'old fox' the questions he had not been able to address. The old fox was the MD himself. Everyone around the room including the secretary of the MD had a good laugh and we settled down to work in a congenial setting. In a similar situation, in many of the Indian companies the export director would have been 'exported' out.

Indian organizations, more so the voluntary ones could do with a little less fear and let joy take its place.

From Power to Persuasion 39

T HAT WILL be the change in the twenty-first century. If the twentieth century belonged to power, this century will belong to persuasion. There are great societal changes taking place around us. And these changes cannot be wished away by organisations.

Managers of today are products of a liberalised era. They are not beholden to past practices. They have not seen the days when for every little thing you had to run to a petty government functionary to get their plans, or their overseas allowances approved by an RBI clerk. They now carry international credit cards. They see themselves not as mere employees but as individualized corporations, which bring on the table a value commensurate with what the corporations seeking to hire their services offer. They take risks unlike most people of my generation. If they are not happy, they just switch jobs. Many of them are two-income families. They have the staying power to wait until something worth *their* while comes along. In all, they are more confident of themselves than their parents.

If we accept this premise, it follows that in the current century, the power of position or authority will just not work. I believe that in the future, it will be the power of persuasion that leaders will need to apply to align their people to the purpose of their organisations.

What kind of changes will we be seeing? Organisations will become much more democratic and participative. Democratic not in terms of 'one person-one vote' but the right to participate and offer views in decision making will be an accepted norm. And that is turn, will lead to greater transparency and less arbitrariness in management functions. The future managers will want their need to be fully met by the organisations they choose to work for.

There will be room for much greater constructive discontent. Diversity in people and ideas will be cherished, instead of being frowned upon. Leaders will aim to convert antagonism into creative energy. They will pay heed to the wisdom expressed by William Wrigley when he says, 'When two people in business always agree, one of them is unnecessary'. *Tell me more* will be the refrain of leaders. If only the mind has ruled in the past, the heart will find its rightful place in the future. People would like to actively seek opportunities to grow. There will be much greater respect for individuals. You will get to hear more *thank yous*.

If there is a large mismatch between the organisation's values and the personal values, leaders will seek alignment between the two. They will seek to determine the collective will of the people on a continual basis.

Watertight legal contracts will have less importance. These will be kept simple to meet legal needs. People will live by common covenants of conduct. Relationships between people will cut across hierarchy and there will be fluidity in the organisational structure. There will be much greater sharing and intimacy in organisations. Leaders will be addressed by their first names. The use of Mr/Ms will decline. There will be greater civility in interpersonal dealings. In the future, you will see more roving leaders depending on *that* situation, in *that* context.

Money will play its part but that will not be the sole driving force. They will seek to actualise themselves in their workplace. The last century saw the domination by Theory X managers, who believed that people will do the least possible to get along in organisations and that the carrot and stick policy was the way to make them work. This century will see the preponderance of Theory Y managers, who believe that most people come to work to do their best and if they cannot achieve it, some organisational hurdle is coming in their way. They will identify the obstacles in consultation with their people and use their privileged position to remove the hurdles.

Leaders will work to harmonise the efficiency of machines with the effectiveness of people. We will see more outstanding groups than outstanding individuals. Leaders of the past inflicted pain on their people when things did not go their way. Leaders of the future will bear pain in identical circumstances. The leaders will ask their people to clarify their (people's) expectation of them. The effort will be in building synergy.

It is likely that at this stage, there might be some readers who may be wondering whether I am not being carried away by a flight of imagination. These readers have a right to know more about the solid basis of my reading of the future.

One explanation that I can offer is that the young will not accept any other way. The old order will make room for the new. And where do I get these insights? From the noisy pubs of Bangalore, when I overhear their conversations, when I hear the new idiom of their language. When I observe the ability of the young to see the bigger picture, overlooking the small irritants the politicians of the country cause on a day-to-day basis. It is in these pubs that I witness a quiet revolution in education that is taking place.

Could it be beer-induced fantasies these young people are indulging in? I believe not. I see them equally intense about their work as they are about their beer. When I look for clues in their past, the majority comes from modest backgrounds. The majority has roots in small towns and rural areas. The majority of them made it good because their parents invested in education, and in most cases, at great personal cost. These youngsters made the most of the educational opportunities offered to them.

The future will see some other changes. Less time will be spent on strategy formulations. The pace of change will be so fast that there will be no relevance of even medium-term strategy. The focus will be on the strong and agile implementation of continually evolving strategy.

Another doubt may appear in the mind of the readers. What about Enron? What about Arthur Anderson? The writer is talking about a perfect organisational world. The real organisational world is different. It is a mean, dog-eat-dog world out there. The companies mentioned above are aberrations.

They are not role-model companies. They are in the news for the wrong reasons. The companies that have delivered long-term value to their stakeholders rest on the pillars of ethical value systems.

Did I hear someone say, *Amen?* If this reads more like a prayer than a prediction, so be it. Then let us all pray for its fruition.

Can Profit-making Organisations be Spiritual? 40

THIS QUESTION came to mind as I read an invitation to a seminar from the Bangalore Management Association on spirituality and organisational transformation.

On a personal level, I see no conflict between business and spirituality. In fact, I would like to see a greater convergence between the two.

I suspect that one of the reasons that the subject of spirituality is not mentioned or discussed in the business environment, is that it is often misunderstood as religiousness. When the R word creeps in, then you start smelling agarbattis, you hear temple or church bells, and the subject of spirituality becomes out-of-bounds. I discovered an example of spirituality in business which I have narrated below:

Our gas stove was not sparking, so we called the company to have it repaired. The service representative promptly showed up and began to work with such total concentration and focus that I felt drawn to watch him. So, I sneaked into the kitchen every now and then to watch him work. The man was completely preoccupied and was whistling while he worked. The cup of coffee that had been served to him was untouched. At the end of his task, he called me into the kitchen and demonstrated how the system was working properly. He explained to me what had gone wrong and told the cook the precautions that ought to be taken in the future. He gave me his card and told me with a smile that he was just a telephone call away, in case he was needed again. When I pointed the cup of coffee that had turned cold, he said, 'Oh'.

To me, this was spirituality at work. The service operator was totally aware of his responsibility towards his company and its customers. Spirituality is about being aware of what is happening within and around us.

You may have observed that one of the most prized and unquestioned attributes of great organisations is service. Their belief is that their profits are a consequence of the service they provide. They put a lot of energy in giving great service to their customers, their shareholders, and their employees and as they gain experience, they find that they receive loyalty in return. Their profits increase. They have better repeat customer record. What else is service if it is not spirituality?

I once worked for a very empathic leader. We were discussing some business issues when he received an emergency call from one of the shops to inform him that a terrible accident had occurred. We both rushed to the site to see that a young manager had severely burnt his arm in an electric oven. This young man was a picture of pain and agony. I saw tears of empathy rolling down the CEO's eyes as he helped him into the ambulance. He visited him in the hospital, provided help to the family and made inquiries after him until the young man returned to work. He was the first person to greet him, and after sharing a cup of tea with him on his first day back at work, walked him down to the manager's office. What else is empathy if it is not spirituality?

There are leaders who are constantly digging out dirt (read defective processes) in their companies. They want to replace the muck with a clean environment (read improved processes). Defective processes, which produce defective products and services, are nothing but dirt for them. Then they set about improving their processes with the help of their people. They don't blame people for wrong results. They hunt for trouble-making processes rather than troublesome people. They recognise that it is only through happy, well-adjusted people that they can hope to have happy, satisfied customers.

Spiritual business leaders create an environment and context of work in which people can realise their maximum potential. Having set the right context, they get out of the way and expect the best from those people. They judge the performance and not the people and are fair when it comes to promotions and rewards. They let it be known that there is no place in their companies for corridor deals. To me, fairness itself is a sign of spirituality.

They are *karmayogis,* concentrate on the process rather than the results. They lead their organisations through personal examples of hard work, sincerely believing that hard work will be rewarded. When you seek an explanation from them, they point your attention to the supreme laws of nature, which among other things, say, that there can be delay but that there will be justice. They also believe that breaking the laws of nature invites much greater wrath than breaking man-made laws.

A premier organisation in Bangalore has set up a counselling centre at their premises. In this centre, people who cannot cope with the extraordinary stress their work and competitiveness places on them, can seek confidential counselling to reaffirm their worth, self-esteem and regain their confidence.

Haven't you met some leaders who, when you go to them with a problem that has been weighing on your mind, make you sit comfortably? They let you say your piece without interruption, they lean back in their chairs, and shut their eyes in concentration and contemplation. And when you leave their rooms, somehow that *big* problem does not look all that tricky and burdensome. They share their experience of similar situations, or recall a parable, and you return feeling able to handle the crisis. This sort of complete focus is yet another sign of spiritual business leaders.

Over lunch with senior people in a company, the conversation drifted to the kind of management books they enjoyed reading, and their favourite management gurus. Some said Peter F. Drucker. Others argued that the Indian-born management authors like C.K. Prahalad and Sumantra Ghosal made better sense to them. In support of their choice, they said that these two authors were familiar with the Indian psyche, and cultural and social ethos, as well as being experts in their field of specialisation.

Then one of them said that he found that the best management book that he had read was The *Bhagwad Gita*. He said with some passion, that he could find most solutions to business conflicts in the *Gita*. I waited for the reaction of the others and noticed some of them nodding in agreement. For good measure he asked his colleagues, 'Where do you think the wisdom of these authors come from?'

This may be the time to narrate a part of the mythical journey described in a renowned book titled *Journey to the East,* by an equally famous German author, Herman Hesse. The author talks of a spiritual journey from Germany to China via India. The group is travelling through the vast and hostile desert of Arabia. Accompanying them is a servant named Leo.

As the journey progresses, the tempers of the spiritual seekers are frayed. They cannot stand the heat and the dust storms, travails and tribulations of this extremely harsh journey. They become irritable with each other. And before the problem becomes too great, Leo somehow appears on the scene, says and does something whereby the group begins to feel good which helps the expedition to proceed. One day, without any notice, Leo, the servant, disappears. As the expedition progresses, the members of the group are on each other's throat. They start deserting the group one by one, and soon, the expedition is abandoned.

One of the participants of the expedition decides to look for Leo. One day while he is coming out of a church, he sees Leo and decides to follow him. He finds Leo entering a monastery and on inquiry, he discovers that Leo was in fact the head of the monastery that had launched the expedition. Leo was a servant first and then a leader.

Many business leaders have successfully modelled their management philosophy on this concept of servant leadership.

In my mind, service, empathy, focus on the process rather than results, respect and concern for the safety of others are spiritual aspects of a person and these cannot be divorced from businesses, which have aims higher than mere profit.

Mind their Minds 41

ALL HELL breaks loose if a couple of CNC machines break down in a manufacturing company, or if a few computers are rendered useless in a software company. But the mental breakdown of the people in a company goes mostly unnoticed. I am not referring here to those who are at the bottom rung of Maslow's hierarchy of needs, struggling to make both ends meet, rather, to those who have everything going for them, especially the top-notch category.

I suspect that the reason for this indifference is that there is very little awareness in the corporate sector on the subject of mental health. The financial losses suffered due to low, or non-performing individuals go unnoticed. And believe me, there is a huge loss in terms of both financials and the avoidable pain caused by emotional trauma. If human capital is an appreciating asset, as most business leaders today acknowledge, this asset must not be allowed to depreciate through deteriorating mental health.

This chapter is an attempt to create awareness of the rudiments of mental health in the corporate sector. Once we understand the problem, only then can we start looking at the solutions.

The first step the management needs to take is to bring the subject of mental health out into the open and destigmatise it. Despite all that has been said and done so far, there is still a lot of hesitancy amongst us about mental illness. The day I will admit to my friends that I am seeing a psychiatrist is far. The best way to achieve this is to invite qualified counsellors to speak about mental health.

Once people in an organisation know how common the malady is, they are less likely to be secretly suffering. The subject needs to be kept in focus through dissemination of information in company newsletters/bulletins. A discussion of case studies also helps because people can identify the illnesses easily.

My experience shows that besides the people in the organisation who are directly affected, even those who are in good mental health may have someone in their families who is suffering. The emotional trauma in a home can have a terrible effect on family members.

The second step is for the management to sufficiently educate themselves on the subject, so that they are able to detect early signs of mental illness, and are able to arrange help without wasting time. Some of these maladies are detailed below to provide a preliminary understanding of the subject:

Depression: This illness is so common that it is beginning to be a universal problem. It ranges from a low feeling to totally dysfunctional behaviour. Many symptoms will provide a red alert. Some include the deterioration of personal hygiene, and declining energy and concentration levels. Since these people do not have much to look forward to, they begin to absent themselves frequently from work, or start coming late. Anger is an integral part of the personality of the depressed person. They tire easily and they complain about being treated poorly. When they are treated with warmth, they cannot return it. The risk of suicide is high among them.

In some cases, you might notice signs that are exactly the opposite. Such people have sudden bursts of energy, and work obsessively till late at night. They may sometimes make incoherent statements. They tire people around them because they never seem to get tired themselves. This form of depression is called manic, or bipolar depression. Statistically, 2 per cent of Indians at the workplace may suffer from depression; 1 per cent of these from manic depression. A lot of corporate people have bipolar illness but because of the stigma involved no one admits it and the illness goes untreated. This is regrettable because depression is a very treatable illness. Medical intervention is absolutely necessary. Additionally, such people may need the support of an experienced counsellor.

Anxiety: The poet, W.H. Audin, describes ours to be an age of anxiety. We are all anxious at some time or the other. A healthy fear protects us, for example, from danger. It is suitable in many of our interactions with persons or events around us. However, sometimes anxiety can pierce through normalcy and become so debilitating that it has an adverse effect on the performance of people in an organisation. Typically, persons who are experiencing an anxiety neurosis feel some kind of uncomfortable dread and apprehension. They believe that there is a nameless threat awaiting them. Their blood pressure and pulse rate increases and they may break into a sweat because they are so anxious about the success of an impending task. Victims of anxiety cannot explain their difficulty in an orderly way. Anxiety can disappear by itself, or it can turn phobic. In a home situation, a father or mother may suffer from a bout of extreme anxiety if the school bus carrying their children is 5–10 minutes late. Anxious people need immediate help from a counsellor who, in some cases, may refer them to a doctor.

Passive Aggressiveness: Some psychiatrists will tell you that passive aggressiveness is the most common disability in an organisation. Persons in authority may be puzzled by these people, who appear too difficult to understand. Although they do not exhibit aggression overtly, they cause no less irritation to those around them. Their passive style is elusive. They may exhibit it by coming late for a meeting planned much in advance, or drop out of an important discussion at the last minute. They may take too long to reply to letters and emails. It is this kind of behaviour that lands them in conflict with their colleagues at work. They seem to hurt people without trying to. They do not build lasting relationships.

One very interesting case that I experienced was a manager who, to get even with the management, would despatch consignments to the wrong destinations and often throw away important letters in the dustbin.

These are people who definitely need counselling.

Obsessive Compulsive: These people want everything to be orderly. They hate surprises. They will rehearse their notes and their presentations many times over, and keep asking their subordinates/colleagues to add this, and delete that, wearing people out by asking for a mass of irrelevant details. They know how to waste their time and that of the others around them. They are particularly sensitive to any from of criticism or feedback. Being quiet and sulking is their best revenge. They are generally intellectual in nature and are constantly revising drafts to find the right word to indicate their dissatisfaction with the one that may have been chosen. They rarely mention anything in the first person but intellectualise and express their feelings in abstract terms. Such people may say that they had some misunderstanding with a colleague, when in fact it was a full-blown verbal bout. They hide their emotions behind intellectual expressions. You will hear them say, 'Well to be honest with you . . .' or, 'To tell you the truth . . . .'

It is unlikely that they will tell you something honestly or truthfully. Such people build systematic defences around them.

This is a broad overview on mental health. The psychology of people in an organisation needs to be understood more closely than we are doing today.

My counselling philosophy precludes giving any direction but I will make an exception. My advice to the senior management is to devote some time to the area of mental health of their people. The Return On Investment (ROI), price earning (PE) ratios, Employee Related Expenses (ERE), sales ratios and other financial indices are important but let us not forget that it is the people who make these ratios possible.

In short: mind the 'mentex' of your company more closely than you mind the Sensex.

The Karma of Business ... and the Business of Karma

42

YOU CAN hang me upside down. You can boo me. You can call me a phony spiritualist and you can even call me names until the cows come home but you *cannot* dissuade me from the belief that the karma of business will soon visit us. You can be sure that the laws of nature (karma) apply in full force, regardless of how high and mighty we are in the corporate world.

I say this with such total conviction because I have seen it in one too many cases to believe otherwise. Given below are some instances of this belief:

A company in the south launched itself in the aviation business with a lot of fanfare. It took a number of aircraft on lease from a foreign leasing company. I was involved with this company as a consultant. During one such visit, I heard the top man telling his finance manager to 'settle the accounts with the b*****d and let him go home. Tell him that I do not ever want to see his face again.' 'These pilots are no better than prostitutes,' he told me with the pride of a haughty man who sat in a mighty position.

A little later, he wanted to cut a deal with me, which meant a slight overlooking here and there of safety issues; there were spoils to be shared.

Another visit, a similar scene. This time, someone was being asked to rub his nose (and say it in writing) if he wanted to be taken back after the summary dismissal the boss man had ordered. After one more visit, another such scene was the last straw.

There was a lot of business to be done with this growing company but we refused to sup with them. Our company concluded that a company, whose top man believed that he could destroy careers in a jiffy, who was willing to jeopardise air safety, would take us to the cleaners one day.

Cut to the future. The company folded up. The creditors hounded out the promoters. The pilots found placements in new companies in the aviation business. Their business associates lost millions of rupees in unsettled accounts. And it took only three years for all this to happen.

That's the business of karma for you.

In another case, there was a large group with a number of associate companies making complimentary and synergic products. One company supported the other and the entire group flourished. They had an unbroken record of profits and dividend payments. The reserves were high and the market valuation soars. This was the story for two generations.

The problems start because egos get in the way. Who is smarter than the other is the question. Who is older than the other is the issue. Who is supporting more than the other is the scorecard. Suspicion replaces trust and becomes the basis of functioning. Fights start. *I go my way, you mind your own business*, is the byword. Gradually, the business is diverted to the competition. Each cuts the nose of the other and spites his own face. The sales drop. The profits drop even more steeply. The sales offices are closed one by one. Assets are sold. The banks are after the blood of the promoters. The owners' majority shares worth millions are not worth the computer they are dematted on. There is sadness all around.

This is the karma of business at work.

The last instance involves me. I met two partners dealing in very large electric motors. They promised to bring in high value business from competition to my company. They delivered on their promise. Business flourished for both of us.

My business friends, however, warned me that I was dealing with a couple of crooks. I replied that I was being paid for my products, so what was the problem? Then they told me that the money owed to the previous supplier was being recycled to pay us for the new business. A good friend saw me with the couple in a restaurant when I was entertaining them as customers. He warned me but I ignored his advice. I took the warning of my friend as business jealousy.

The partners tell me that they have a trust from where they fund charities. They give money for a charity for which I am a trustee. They have my trust and I have theirs. However, during all this, something troubles me but I ignore my inner voice.

One day, I get a call from one of them. I am now on a *bhai sahib* basis with them. They ask me to send a large consignment to Ahmedabad. What about the payment, I ask. No problem, they say. They will be coming on Sunday evening with the bank draft but '*bhai sahib,* do dispatch the goods because there is a heavy penalty involved.' I do exactly that. I dispatch the equipment.

One partner decides to fall ill on that fateful Sunday morning. The trip is postponed by a couple of days, then by another few days for yet another reason.

When I ask for payment, they even get angry with me. 'We have done business with you for such a long time and have been paying up on time. One little delay and you are getting impatient?' The respectful phrase *bhai sahib* is missing now in their conversation.

Then they stop receiving my calls. They are travelling abroad. Yes, the message will be passed to them. I am under pressure from within the company for realising Rs 400,000 from the two crooks. Whom can I blame? People I trust had warned me to stay away from them. I did not listen. I did not listen to myself. I was greedy for business. As a result, the company suffered a heavy loss.

And I suffered a loss of face. Fortunately, I was senior enough to condone myself but anyone less fortunate would have got the sack.

This was business of karma at play.

Cases like these, not only from my business life but also from my airforce days are abundant.

What happened to that Joe Varma who was going places and who used to mock us for working so hard while he picked up better reports by doing this or that for the bosses? He retired only as a wing commander; it seems he got into some trouble and had to face a loss of seniority. Another was superseded and had to serve out his time without any further promotion.

There may be some who say that there are so many business crooks who have got away with murder and others still are roaming around with immunity...

Well, we can quarrel on the time frame for karma to play its role but not as to the universality of it.

Reengineer Yourself before Reengineering Corporations

43

THE BANGALORE Management Association, in coordination with the Sambodh Foundation, conducted a one-day seminar on 'Spirituality and Leadership for Organisational Transformation'. Swami Bodhananda, the spiritual leader of the Sambodh Foundation, was the lead speaker at the seminar.

The most impressive feature about the Swami was his comprehensive understanding of the corporate sector, the market realities, the issues connected with globalisation and the harsh realities of the traditional management approach that Indian corporations continue to follow.

He appreciated that India needed to create wealth to overcome the curse of poverty and become an economic power, failing which nations that are more powerful will call the shots and keep India economically dependent.

In this chapter, I have drawn heavily on a very small part of the many wise and practical suggestions he made to his audience, which included mostly working managers.

He said that the efforts towards re-engineering corporations would fail, unless the process of re-engineering began with the self. How does one begin this process of re-engineering?

He invited the audience to look at some new paradigms. These are:

Moving from 'I am a physical body' attitude to 'I am a spirit' attitude

We must believe that we are spiritual beings in physical bodies and, therefore, poses limitless possibilities.

His mantra was, if you are looking for a mantra, to say to yourself, *I am Shiva. I was born as Shiva.* Chanting this mantra in the morning will help you change your self-image. We are what we think we are. In his inimitable style, he reminded the audience that he was parting with high technology without any cost and without any side effects. Make *I am Shiva* your morning mantra.

Inside out

If we accept the premise that we are not mere physical beings, then we will see our growth from inside out, like a seed-to-a-tree growth. Just as a seed has to be nurtured to grow into a healthy tree, we are required to nurture ourselves through self-validation, self-love and a positive image. If we consider ourselves to be a poor specimen of humanity, then humanity is not likely to disagree with our own assessment of ourselves.

The Swami added that everything starts with intentions. These generate thoughts, which are expressed in words, leading to deeds. Deeds performed regularly become our habits, which shape our character, and eventually, that becomes our destiny. We can control our destiny by selecting our intentions.

If our intentions are of giving, then self-giving becomes our character. It is only after giving that we truly qualify to receive. The economics of spirituality is that the more we give, the more we receive. 'First give, then take', should be our motto, advised Swami Bodhananda. That is the way to realise our maximum potential. Anything less, and we would shortchange ourselves.

Challenge and Response

The world is constantly throwing challenges at us. What kind of response we give to those challenges is strictly in our domain. We have the ultimate choice to respond positively and enthusiastically, or have a *chalta hai* attitude. We must never forget that the right to choose our response lies with us. With this belief, if nothing else, we will stop blaming others for our miseries and failures. We will get rid of the *my boss, my neighbour,* and *my wife* syndrome. The first tendency is to run away from unpleasant situations. The unfortunate part is that these situations do not go away. They revisit us with greater force and greater effect.

The Swami did not agree with those who want to hide from the world and run away to Rishikesh to escape the responsibilities of life.

To celebrate ourselves, he said, one does not have to wait for big victories. We should celebrate our daily victories, however small they may be. The challenge and response technique should be used as an important tool for self-control, was the sage advice from the sage.

Detached Engagement

This actually means having a non-reactive response to your work. If you begin to inculcate the expectation of an outcome to your work but not react to the outcome expected, over a period of time, you will begin to develop equanimity. You will then be able to integrate success and failure.

A good example of detached engagement is the tennis star Andre Agassi. When he is playing tennis, he plays with detached engagement. He is not constantly looking at the score board, or frowning when it moves against him. He doesn't jump with joy when it moves in his favour. He knows that he has to concentrate on the process of playing. The movement of the score board is a consequence of his detached engagement and not the other way around.

Happiness is Here and Now

The Swami explained that without a doubt, we are the embodiment of happiness. We do not have to work for happiness. It is an integral part of our being, and if we are not happy, we have chosen it that way.

Blaming others, or ourselves results in unhappiness. When we start blaming other people, we stop growing. The reason we blame others, is that when we are busy doing that, we do not have the time to look at ourselves. Perhaps we are afraid that by being more aware of our own behaviour, we might end up discovering nasty things about ourselves. Blaming other people is a handy avoidance technique.

Spirituality essentially is contemplation, introspection, awareness and prayer. To access that dimension we have to discipline ourselves but sadly, most people are not keen to access that dimension and choose to stay put in a perpetual rut.

Lest readers begin to believe that it is easy for swamis to give these lectures, disappear in a cave to meditate and wait for the disciples to turn up with fruits and flowers, you just have to look at the vast list of the activities of Swami Bodhananda.

Going by the routine that he keeps and the number of organisations he supervises, here in India and abroad, the Swami's responsibilities appeared to be no less than those of a CEO of a large corporation.

In his opening address, he made it clear that materialism and spirituality were not mutually exclusive concepts.

For example, try practising meditation on an empty stomach. I would be happy if you shared your experience with me. Speaking for myself, on an empty stomach, my mind wanders from a bunch of bananas to the box of biscuits and the lone Alfonso mango my wife just could not eat the previous night.

And I forget the *I am Shiva* mantra.

Conversations with a CEO 44

Dear CEO,

GREETINGS FROM a former chief executive! Now that I have your undivided attention, I'd like to take this opportunity to share some experiences and insights, gained over 40 years of corporate life. For the purpose of this conversation, do keep in mind that any person, who is in charge of any resource, big or small, is a chief executive.

An important confession I have to make is that in the past 40 years, I was responsible for a fair amount of the mess that was invariably created wherever I worked. The learning process of cleaning up the mess taught me many things.

I have often wondered whether CEOs become too preoccupied with the hard side of management. By this, I mean that we spend disproportionate amounts of time in dealing with the selection of machines and material, making our best people responsible for these resources. We want to know the serviceability, the raw material content, the efficiency figures of the machines we are buying and selling, the costs involved, and the machine outputs. We look at the percentages in our financial results with total concentration and analyse variations from our intended objectives, to put remedial measures in place.

Although these are important issues and must receive our attention, I sometimes think we forget our only appreciating asset—our people. What if we understood that only 25 per cent of our workforce perform to their total potential! And that about 33 per cent of employees do barely enough work to stay out of trouble! I bet that there would be hell to pay if we got these kinds of results from our machines!

It is a fact that in our organisations, there are a lot of people who have very low self-esteem, who suffer from anxiety, have relationship problems, are mildly depressed, feel unappreciated, and suffer from a host of other human frailties. These people cry out for help in many ways, through their body language, by the tone and tenor of their conversation, the level and quality of their participation, and even their unsure entry into our rooms. In short, they send out enough signals for us to be aware that they are unhappy.

As CEOs, we need to develop enough sensitivity to spot these troubled employees. People want to be understood. Similarly, employees with personal problems look for an understanding of their problems and usually just need a kind word, some encouragement and the confidence that they will be heard without being judged as *less than they are*. An assurance that their boss will be there to walk the journey with them will go a long way to improved performance and morale. It should be noted that comparisons with others in similar circumstances do not work, nor do pep talks. People's problems are unique to them. With a little bit of patience and a lot of understanding and compassion at the workplace, employees will begin to feel better about their lives. Simultaneously, you will see a gradual but distinct improvement taking place in their work, which will also energise them towards better overall performance. It's that simple.

It took me many years and a very candid remark from an employee to realise that the best answer to a problem comes from those who are close to it. This employee said something like this: '*Sahib*, if only these managers bothered to ask us how to set a problem right at our workstation, they wouldn't be running around like mad dogs looking for solutions.' Strong words indeed, but it is hard to question the logic behind this statement.

Yes, we believe we have solutions for everything. It is my belief that it is very important to involve those who are closest to the problem in decision making. If you do this, you will not have to chase the solution to the problem. Employees will feel responsible for solving the issue at hand. You will be inundated with suggestions to help resolve problems. In fact, you will realise that your organisation will find it difficult to implement all the suggestions, and they will have to be prioritised.

Another very important thing to keep in mind is that you should always remember your employees on important occasions—*their* important occasions.

Both happy and sad. If you are invited to a wedding, *go*. If you have to attend a funeral, the same applies. It is *not* a waste of your busy time. You *cannot* delegate empathy. You need to express it personally. A little of your time in their hour of happiness or sadness fetches you the most rewards on the time that you invest. Remember also to delegate your most sensitive people to deliver any compensation that may be due to the employee or his family at his residence. And tell your finance man to shut up if he quotes the rulebook. So, postpone that board meeting for two hours—it will not make any difference to your company's future. But it *will* make a lot of difference to how people feel about you and through you, your company.

There are many CEOs who write letters of appreciation to deserving employees. However, sadly, most of these letters are so stereotyped and lacking in emotion that the recipient knows that you have only performed a duty and does not really feel appreciated. Write a *genuine, straight-from-the heart* letter, saying how well he or she has conducted himself/herself and how they have made the company proud by their performance. Describe the event in a few words. When you write a genuine letter, the emotion is apparent and will be noticed. They will make copies of your letter, file it in their personal papers and show it to their families with great pride.

That company newsletter that is circulated should not be for your pictures. CEOs have no place in it. Instead, this place belongs to your employees and their families. Have their children draw on-the-spot paintings on your lawns and let their toddlers have a wonderful time. Run with them on the company's annual day—don't just flag off the run. And try not to come first! Participation is very important because it make them feel you are one of them.

I'm sure you think that all this sounds like very 'soft' advice—but learning soft 'people' skills is very often hard to do. And do well.

Good luck!

A Leader or a Detractor? 45

THAT IS the question we all need to ask of ourselves, to establish how high and how far we will go in an organisation—as well as in our lives.

Robert R. Carkhuff, a renowned psychiatrist and best-selling author of several books on human performance, suggests that people function at five different levels of performance.

The lowest level is observed amongst detractors, who are the kind to essentially find fault with any human endeavour. If a refreshing and tasty cup of soup is prepared for them, they will take great pleasure in declaring that some ingredient is missing. They are impoverished physically, emotionally and intellectually. Thus, they do not add value to any effort but do everything to subtract from it, or at best, stay uninvolved. Dr Carkhuff categorises them as those who are under-resourced, underprivileged and disfranchised.

Next are the observers, or the passive spectators of a game being played. They can be described as people who are on the fringes of civilised behaviour. How do we recognise an observer? Give them an incentive and they will work. However, they will hold themselves back from any active participation or any direct involvement. They are largely dependent people. The majority of people come under this category.

Climbing up another step of the ladder are the players, or the participants. They are physically adaptive, responsive to others around them, and are keen to achieve something in their lives. Since it is in their nature to participate, they share, explore and are achievement-oriented. According to Carkhuff, fully participative people are a rare species these days.

Rarer still are those on the next level—the contributors. This species not only become whole-heartedly involved in any endeavour they undertake but also continuously add value to the job in hand. Such people bring about a freshness in their approach and are capable of 'out-of-the-box' or creative thinking.

Contributors appear physically intense, on the path of self-actualisation, are confident and there-fore, are able to act in an interdependent mode. They can understand the feelings and the thoughts of their colleagues, and are emotionally and intellectually competent people. This sort of person leaves an im-print of his/her personality and is able to make a difference in the work undertaken, or to other people's lives.

According to Dr Carkhuff, this is an essential personality attribute before aspiring to take on the last step on the ladder—the step to leadership.

If you have been a contributor, the next logical step is towards being a leader. Leaders are people who dig in their heels, are physically enduring and mission-oriented. They are high on the scale of initiatives and are adept at interpersonal skills. They are also able to offer breakthrough solutions.

How does one get to the top of the ladder? I am afraid there are no short-cut solutions to making progress. The best way is to first establish examine where you presently fit it. Are you a detractor, observer, participant, or a contributor? It is essential to know where you are before going where you want to go. Some people regard themselves as mission-oriented and thus think they are entitled to leadership but there is no way you can skip these key stages in human development.

Clearly admit to yourself the stage of development you are at. That is the most essential step. If we do not know our inadequacies and are not willing to admit them as our personal infirmities, there is not much room to move forward. Accepting ourselves as we are is a liberating thought and it is out of this thought that the power to move ahead comes, in order to identify what the next step to progress is.

This requires continuous mapping in a measurable way. We can then set standards and objectives, develop action plans to achieve them, review these plans on a regular basis, and place ourselves on the road to personal development.

One thing is certain—we do not have to remain stagnant. It is in the nature of all organisms to evolve further. Settling for anything less than that would mean we are short-changing ourselves. We owe ourselves a better deal than we often offer.

Servant Leadership 46

I INVITE the reader to enter into a new paradigm of thinking on the subject of leadership. Hopefully, this will set in motion two things: (*a*) a personal inquiry in each one of us as to what real leadership is all about; and *(b)* possibly generate a debate whether our organisations and leaders are ready to adopt this style of leadership. It is clear that the traditional and hierarchical style of management will just not work in the twenty-first century. The style of management that is likely to succeed is the one that enhances the growth of people working in the company, through a combination of team work, personal involvement in decision making and ethical and caring behaviour.

The term *servant leadership* was first coined in 1970 by Robert Greenleaf (1904–90). He worked for AT&T for 40 years and thereafter, he enjoyed a second career spanning 25 years as a very influential consultant. His understanding of the concept of servant leadership became crystallised when he read a short novel, *Journey to the East*, written by a German author, Herman Hesse. The book is an account of a mythical journey by a group of people on a spiritual quest. The central figure in this story is a character called Leo, who accompanies the party as a servant and who sustains them with a caring spirit.

All is going well with the expedition until one day Leo disappears. The group quickly falls into disarray, and the journey is abandoned. The group just cannot manage without Leo. After many years of searching, the narrator of the story stumbles upon Leo and is taken into the religious order that sponsored the original journey. There, he discovers that Leo, whom he had known as a servant, was in fact the head and the guiding spirit of the order. Leo was a great servant and a noble leader.

This servant leadership model puts serving others including employees, customers, the community, the society, and shareholders as the number one priority. It begins with the feeling that one wants to serve first, and in the wake of desire to serve, comes an aspiration to lead. Like Leo, who was a perfect servant first, to become a perfect leader. The difference emerges in the fact that a servant leader first wants to make sure that other people's highest priority needs are being met, whether these are our employees, customers, shareholders or community members.

And how does he know whether this is happening in his organisation?

The best test, according to Greenleaf is, do those who are being served grow as persons; do they, while being served, become healthier, wiser, freer, more autonomous and in the process become servant leaders themselves? It is important to stress at this stage itself that servant leadership is not a quick-fix approach. Nor is it something that can be quickly instilled within an institution. At the core of it, servant leadership is a long-term transformational approach to work. Not only to work but to life itself. It is a way of being and doing that has the potential to create a positive change within the organisation.

When you go through Greenleaf's original writing and the commentaries written by other authors on the concept of servant leadership, 10 critical characteristics emerge in a servant leader. These are listed below:

Listening: This is the first critical characteristic. Servant leaders have a deep commitment to listening intently to others. Through this process of intense listening, they seek to clarify the will of a group. For them, it is very important to know the will of the people, for they know that unless people in an organisation willingly get enrolled in an idea, nothing great can be achieved. They not only listen intently to others, but also to their inner voices. Listening and reflection at regular intervals are the key to the growth of servant leaders. The biggest barrier to listening is the difference between the rate of speaking and the rate at which we think. We think four times faster than we speak. So, there is plenty of time when some one is talking to us to get distracted and take side trips that reduce the percentage of the message actually received. Servant leaders do not allow themselves to be distracted. And they listen without making judgements.

Empathy: It is not enough for servant leaders to listen intently but to listen with empathy. A servant leader might reject someone's behaviour or viewpoint but he will never reject him as a person. People need to be accepted as they are. The most successful servant leaders are those who have become skilled empathetic listeners. In this process of empathetic listening, the listener becomes totally aligned to the person he/she is listening to.

Healing: The next critical characteristic of a servant leader is healing. There are many broken spirits roaming around in our organisations, suffering from a variety of emotional hurts. These people have latent abilities that are very high, but they continue to perform much below their true potential, simply because their spirits are broken. Servant leaders recognise this problem in their employees and set about healing them. They help people to recover their self-esteem and confidence in themselves. It always amazes me to see how top management are so delighted with the performance of their equipment that they have no time to establish the performance of their people. If they only knew, that on an average, 75 per cent do not perform to their potential and at least 33 per cent admit to doing barely enough to stay out of trouble.

Servant leaders help to heal these low performers, to unleash their energy in a positive direction. In the process of healing, their stand is *I enable you and empower you through my love and my patience and my firmness. I love you enough not to let you do less than your best. However, I don't shame you into it. I invite you into it.*

Awareness: Servant leaders are keenly aware of themselves and of what the ethics and values involved in an issue are. Being a servant leader can be quite intimidating because making a commitment to foster awareness can also mean that you might hit dirt about yourself and your company. They believe that the cleaning process can start only when the dirt is visible to all. Ethics is the guiding light in all their dealings. Awareness, as we all know, does not guarantee peace. In fact, it disturbs peace. Servant leaders are reasonably disturbed people. They have their own inner security and serenity to cope with any disturbance that awareness brings.

Persuasion: In making and implementing decisions, servant leaders seek to use persuasion rather than the power of their position. They seek to convince and enrol others, rather than enforce compliance. They are very effective in building consensus within a group and within groups. In fact, this is one characteristic they possess that sets them apart from authoritarian leaders. They believe in co-operative rather than combative management. Greenleaf says that coercive power is useful to stop something, or to destroy something but nothing too constructive can be done about it. Persuasion is a better tactic.

Conceptualisation: Servant leaders are dreamers of big dreams. They can think beyond everyday realities. They are not consumed by short-term operational goals. They are visionaries but are very good at striking a fine balance between conceptualisation and day-to-day focus.

Foresight: Servant leaders are very intuitive people. They have the foresight to understand the lessons from the past, the realities of the present and the likely consequences of a decision for the future.

Stewardship: Servant leaders are essentially stewards. Stewardship means holding something in trust for another. The concept of stewardship requires CEOs, directors and senior people always to be conscious of the fact that they are trustees and are holding their institution in trust for the greater good of the society. To be a steward means to be open and persuasive, rather than being controlling and manipulative. Stewardship implies a commitment to serving the needs of others, first and foremost.

Commitment to Personal Growth of Employees: Servant leaders are deeply committed to the personal, professional and spiritual growth of each individual within the organisation. In practice, this can mean making available funds for learning new skills, taking personal interest in employees' ideas/suggestions, encouraging the involvement of everyone in the process of decision making, and actively assisting workers who have been laid off to find other employment. Servant leaders of an engineering company will not hesitate to funding a painting course for an artistic employee, believing that a fully expressed employee will be an asset to the organisation.

Servant leaders also accept failure while building skills for success. It is all right with them for their people to make mistakes. They believe that unless people fail, they are probably not trying hard enough. They are apt to say, 'Believe me; I will back you up. If there is a problem, come to me. I will provide you a safety net.' In this process, they jettison the old top–down hierarchical model and replace it with a servant leader approach. *What value can I add to your work? What hurdles can I remove from your way? What doors can I open for you?* These issues occupy their minds. They turn the traditional concept of leadership on its head and talk in terms of 'span of support' rather than 'span of controls'. Their commitment to the growth of their people is so complete that they are willing to accept unlimited liability on behalf of their people.

Building a Community: Servant leaders realise that large institutions have an obligation in building a sense of community in their people. They understand that collectively, large businesses have more resources at their disposal, greater than all the governments of the globe put together, to cause the difference in building communities around them.

These, then, are the 10 critical characteristics of a servant leader. The concept involves increased service to others, taking a more holistic approach to work, promoting a sense of community within an organisation, sharing of power and decision making, and a group-oriented approach to work in contrast to the hierarchical model.

All this requires commitment, time and energy. It is based on relationships rather than things. It requires courage of conviction and not courage of brashness.

The final test remains the same. And that is: do those served by me grow as persons; do they, while being served, become wiser, freer, more autonomous, more likely to become servants? Is servant leadership a utopian concept, or is it a question of a paradigm shift from our current position on leadership?

I will close this chapter by quoting Robert Greenleaf: 'Caring for persons, the more able and the less able serving each other, is the rock upon which a good society is built.'

Leadership is a Shared Ethical Culture

47

The time is always right to do the right thing.

—Martin Luther King Jr

T HE JURY is out on whether owner-managed companies serve the society better than professionally-managed ones. Other murky areas include issues like whether or not conglomerates are suitable for developing countries, and public versus private ownership in some areas of business.

But one issue that need not wait for a verdict, is that leadership is a shared ethical culture.

It is risky to bring up such an important subject but it can't be wished away. When students pay bribes to teachers to cheat during examinations, when inside trading makes millions for some at the cost of others, when scandals surface on an almost daily basis in the central and state governments, the issue of ethics in leadership must remain in sharp focus.

Somehow, we have begun to believe that ethics and business or governance is mutually exclusive. I believe that ethical leaders are successful leaders. For instance, see the examples of family-run companies in India. While some have survived, others have drowned in the deluge of change. However, there is one common element that can be observed in successful family-run companies—ethics. You will observe that these companies are led with honesty, guided by good values and strong moral principles. You trust these companies. It is also true that those leaders who thought they were the cat's whiskers headed the family-run companies that sank into oblivion.

A study done in the US on the Dow Jones companies, showed conclusively that the companies which became institutions, were the ones that served their stakeholders best year after year and had an ethical code of conduct.

What is ethical and what is not, is a question that needs addressing.

The trouble with the issue of ethics is that often, one knows, can feel and experience what is ethical and what is not but it becomes difficult to explain. An internal compass, whose true north is ethics, guides great leaders. Integrity is their guiding principle. 'A leader is not someone who runs others, but someone who carries water for his people so that they can get on with the jobs.'

Well-known authors, who have dealt with the issue of ethics in leadership at great length, include Ken Blanchard of *The One Minute Manager*, Vincent Peale of *The Power of Ethical Management*, Peter Block of *Stewardship* and Max DePree of *Leadership is an Art*.

Here is a litmus test we could all apply to gauge our attitude to ethics in business. It comes from *The Power of Ethical Management* (Peale):

You are looking for a sales manager and the person who you are interviewing has all the right credentials, experience and knowledge of the industry. He has come from your direct competitor. He is exactly the kind of person you were looking for. And as you are about to shake hands with him at the end of the interview, he takes out a CD and says, 'If you hire me, all the confidential information of my company will come with me.'

What is our reaction? These are the kinds of ethical dilemmas we are often faced with. The issues that will go through our minds will quite likely be: If he can do this to his previous company, he can do the same to mine. If I can do this to my competition, they can do it to me. My God, I am sitting on a goldmine of information, can I let it go? Everything is fair in war and business; it is a dog-eat-dog world. The leader now has a chance to establish a shared culture.

The word will travel down the line sooner than we think. The word will travel fast that you are not walking the walk or talking the talk. Superficially it looks like a soft approach, but ask an ethical leader and he will tell you that what looks soft and slow, is hard and fast. It takes a lot of effort and energy but ethical leaders know that it is well worth it. There is a different quality rate of return that unethical leaders don't know how to measure.

If the decision is to reject the person, people in the company will know what is expected of them. No lectures, no sermons, no exhortations are needed to establish a shared ethical culture. If the decision is to take the person, people will know clearly, that it is expected of them to leave this ethics stuff at the door of their offices or the gates of their factories. Whatever else the leader might say about ethics, they will not believe him.

If you cannot lead yourself by ethical values, you cannot lead someone whom you possibly don't know.

I mentioned a little earlier that it is easier to experience ethics than to explain it. But when we look for some concrete questions for testing the ethics of the situation, we get three or four of them from the collective wisdom of many authors.

Is what I am doing legal, not only from the point of view of the law of the land but also from the covenants of my company? The covenants established over a period are as important as any criminal or civil law.

Is my action fair and balanced? In a corporate set-up, all kinds of questions are asked, but one that is rarely raised, is on the fairness of the decision to all those who will be affected by it in the short and the long run.

It is my belief that if the decision is not a win-win decision, it will boomerang on us. We can quarrel over the time frame, in which it will happen because whatever we might say or believe, the laws of universe apply to us whether we are in pinstripe or night suits.

Will I be able to live by the decision as a person? Will it pinch me? Will it trouble me? How will this decision make me feel about myself?

One question that arises in my mind is the attitude of the employees of a company that adopts unethical practices.

I have seen this demonstrated on several occasions. When an ethical leader is replaced by an unethical one, the same set of people who followed the norms of ethics in the previous regime, calibrate their response when the leadership changes.

At the end of the day, it is all about leadership, isn't it?

It is a funny thing about life; if you refuse to accept anything but the best, you very often get it.

—Somerset Maugham

What Good is Your Strategy if You Cannot Communicate?

48

I DRIFTED into the corporate world from the defence forces. One of the things I found sorely lacking in the corporate world was ability of its managers to communicate lucidly, either verbally or in writing. Perfectly brilliant designers would freeze into a shell when asked to explain their design philosophy to a visiting customer or a potential technical collaborator. The letters that went out of the corporations lacked clarity and conciseness and often confused more than they clarified. Nearly all sales letters, after a visit to the customers, would take a form like this: *Thank you very much for the courtesy extended to the undersigned during his visit to your works on...,* and end with: *Thanking you in anticipation...*

The letters were boring in content, soulless, lifeless, as if two objects and not two human beings were communicating with each other. The company's in-plant training, instead of recognising this inadequacy and dealing with it head-on, would merely gloss over it. Often, amusing situations were created while dealing with the overseas suppliers and customers when the choice of words and idiom left the two parties seeking endless clarification. The confusion was compounded when the communication was with another non-English speaking country.

It has taken many years for me to understand the root of the problem. The fault lies in the syllabus structure of the B-schools. Some schools don't even include communication as a subject, while others give it such nominal treatment that it is not even worth the mention. There are others who teach the 'mechanics' of written communication like *from*, *to*, *date*, *subject*, etc. The 'electronics' of how to build a rapport with the reader, how to grab his attention and hold him there, how to enroll the person in your idea, how to soothe the nerves of an irate customer, how to win friends and influence people, is ignored.

The questions that keep cropping up in my mind are these. What good is teaching of strategy if you can't explain it clearly to your colleagues and the rank and file? What good are all Philip Kotler's lessons in marketing if you cannot write, a decent letter? What is the point of giving high credit points to strategy when in fact the means of conveying strategy is not even a part of your agenda?

Given the choice, I would like to see a lot more attention given to creating a much higher comfort level with oral and written communication. This could be done by creating imaginary situations and asking them to describe it in their own words. Every student/manager has the right to write, only if we let them exercise that right. Book reading and reviews should be an essential part of the syllabus. The dressing up (mechanical part) they will learn with ease, without much coaching.

To be fair, I must mention that some schools have recognised this basic need and have set up toastmaster's clubs to improve the oral communication level of their students. There are some which have gone ahead and established communication centres in the school with the sole purpose of retrieving lost ground.

Moving away for a moment from the subject of communication to something closely connected with it, is the teaching of etiquette. Indian managers come from different backgrounds—rural and urban, convent educated or from government schools, higher and lower strata of incomes. This disparity needs to be recognised by the schools and the companies. Good communication needs to be backed by good etiquette and grooming in all aspects of a potential manager's life. This would include many things like telephone manners, dress sense, entertaining, being entertained, the art of conversation, behaviour in mixed company, and formal sit-down dinners. Although the norms of etiquette have become a bit more liberal and flexible, good grooming is still a charming aspect of a manager's life, not in superficial terms but as a living part of our personality.

B-schools need to shed their 'product out' policy and adopt a 'market in' approach. Their markets are companies. By the way, when was the last time school officials met companies to establish their needs? Or, when did the companies even think of giving clear 'specifications' of the 'products' they wanted?

The wall between the two must be pulled down through frequent interactions.

If Your Shoes are Not Shining, You Cannot Deliver Quality

49

DOES THIS sound too simplistic? I am of the firm belief that it actually is as simple as the title suggests—if your personal quality needs are not reflected in your shoes, you cannot deliver quality. If it is acceptable for a person to wear dirty shoes, sport frayed collars and an unkempt beard, then it is not likely that he would notice a blob of extra paint, or a chipped corner on the product being shipped out. Quality, like excellence, is not divisible. Quality is all about attitudes.

What would you think of managers who are frequently late for meetings that they have called for themselves? Would they be conscious of delivery schedules of their products?

Personal quality and corporate quality are intertwined like Siamese twins. Point number eight of Dr Deming's *14 Points on Quality* says: 'Drive out fear so that everyone may work effectively for the company'. I believe that the day we start to collect data on our personal defects, we will be that much more aware and effective about how to collect data on defects in products. For instance, if a letter lies on our table without a response for a whole week, chances are that we will miss doing product defect data analysis with our teams, for two weeks.

A manager who is grossly overweight, and has difficulty climbing two flights of stairs to reach his corporate office, is likely to postpone his visit to the shop floors or the sales office to the evening, just before leaving work for the day. It is much too much for him to climb the stairs a second time in one day! Though perhaps a little extreme, this example helps to illustrate my point of view.

Or, for example, you are a visiting a managing director, who during the meeting with you, answers a telephone call and talks to his caller for 15 minutes, making you wait before resuming his conversation with you. Then you observe another who tells his secretary to put all calls on hold till after the meeting with you. You have a choice to do business with either one of them. My choice for the obvious reasons will be the second MD. That little difference in personal quality caused a huge difference.

Point 14 of Deming's philosophy says: 'Put everyone in the company to work to accomplish the transformation. The transformation is everybody's job'.

In a pre-departure briefing with the head of the company, I went through the progress that the company had made between my two visits. The good man made it a point to inform me of all the personal initiatives he had taken in those areas. However, when I started talking about the company's unfinished agenda, he blamed others. Then, while seeing me off at the door, he sighed and said if every one in the company worked as hard as he did, things would be different. Not a great example of personal quality!

It was no wonder then that the process of enthusing others had to wait until a new leader came along to replace the complainer and the blamer. Who will quarrel with the adage: 'Growth stops when the blame starts'?

Companies all over the world are pursuing six sigma standards in quality. Statistically, this means that they are aspiring for defect levels not exceeding three, in 1 million product/service deliveries. In one such company, the chairman made a few pro-forma remarks at the opening ceremony and left. During lunch, the executives of the company exhibited their dedication to new levels of achievement. All of them acknowledge that the *boss* has to be an involved leader if quality is to be a key culture, practice, and result in renewing the companies.

The same Bob Galvin has described in his *Heresies of Quality,* the 'Old Testament' (OT) and the 'New Truths' (NT). The first items on his list are:

OT: Quality control is an ordinary company and department responsibility.

NT: Quality improvement is not just an institutional assignment; it is a daily *personal* obligation.

Need one say more?

Redefining Supervision 50

T HE CONTEXT of business in India has undergone a sea change. The engineering industry, once considered a straggler, is beginning to occupy a place of pride again. Our strength in many areas like IT, biotech and pharmaceuticals is globally recognised. Liberalisation, despite occasional hiccups, is becoming an accepted reality. We are not regarded as pushovers in many businesses.

There is one area, however, where our position continues to be archaic and not in tune with the world we live in. This is in the area of supervision. Most people understand the word 'supervision' as literally meaning that someone is checking on someone else's output and is assessing it mostly with a numerical template. The emphasis is on discovering and pointing out what is not done, rather than what has been done. The emphasis is on the negative and not on the positive.

Not surprisingly, the interpretation of the word 'supervised' is no different. *Watch out, the supervisor is coming this way* or, *Do you think the supervisor or the senior manager will approve of this? Let's not tell him anything. Let's make it difficult for him to discover what has not been done, lest he faults us.* After some time, this mechanical model becomes a routine and it continues more in form than substance. Over time, the system covers a whole basement full of cupboards with these reports, which have been filed for years. I know of one organisation, which seeks supervisory reports on a weekly basis, as if skill changes take place on an hourly basis.

When you go to the root of this malady, you find that this concept or approach to supervision comes from an overhang of our socialist past. This has happened not only in India but also in the other societies that adopted a socialist model, at some point in their history.

In a socialist society, the means of governance are mostly in the hands of the government in power. Take a look at the post-war British socialist era. The government controlled almost all human activity. Whether it was British Airways, British Telecom, or British Rail, education, nursing, hospitals, mining, steel and even psychotherapy was under the purview of the almighty government. The supervisory system, put in place, came from the bureaucratic mindset of a hierarchical command and control structure, where the element of bossiness is ever present. Long after the wave of Thatcherism swept Great Britain, and control moved into the hands of the private sector, the archaic rules continued. The efficiency of doctors was measured by the number of patients seen, rather than the quality of services provided.

A British psychiatrist who was visiting India, confided that after seeing his patients in therapy, he was required to generate a weekly report for his supervisor, who would invariably tell him what had not been done in the therapy. A host of theoretical, textbook solutions would be provided to him while he was going through chaotic sessions, during which his patients were narrating their traumatic experiences. He did not even know what would crop up the next moment. The spontaneity of dialogue was the key to deal with such fluid situations. Even in these areas of human activity, the supervisors were doing a quantitative assessment of the doctors. How many patients were coming back? What were they saying about the doctor?

When I asked how he coped with such an asinine system, he told me that the therapists did everything to improve their patient return data because they knew that is what counted. It was terrible, he said, to be in the counselling room, always aware that Big Brother was watching. Soon, the junior psychiatrists learnt the art of calibrating their responses and reports to please the seniors. Moreover, the system degenerated into a paper-filing exercise.

He added that mercifully, things had recently changed. Supervision for them now meant that if, after a heavy therapy session, you wanted to have a brainstorming session with another colleague, you walked into his office and had an informal dialogue. The colleague also unburdened himself of the pressure generated by his patients. He said they did not even use the term *patient* often. The word now used was *client*. The process began to be called co-counselling, done at the peer level.

I believe the same old British pattern of supervision still exists in India.

Let us now look at what the words 'supervision' and 'supervisor' really mean. Clearly, supervision means 'vision that is superior in quality'. A supervisor therefore, would be someone who has 'super vision' in that area of activity; the first person that would come to your mind, when you were stuck in a situation and needed advice.

It isn't that we don't understand the changes that have taken place in other countries. It is not that we don't know of the latest thinking on the matter. In India, we are always strong on information and data but poor on implementation. But the bigger reason, I suspect, is that there is a certain element of power attached to the present system of supervision. And it is precisely this power that is hard to give up.

Power in the hand of the supervisor helps him to control people and keep them beholden to him. It is with this power that he can demote you, promote you or select what area of learning is best for you.

When I started to look at the process of supervision more closely, I found that most of them were not formally trained to be supervisors. They just got there almost by accident, age or seniority. In many cases, supervisors did not feel adequate or equipped to carry out the process of supervision. And therefore, they chose to strike some kind of cosy relationship between themselves and the supervised, just to perpetuate the system and not rock the boat.

I believe that the time has come to lift this façade and substitute it with a system, which is more co-counselling in its nature like the visiting psychiatrist mentioned has been introduced in Great Britain. We need a system in which a dialogue between the supervisor and the supervised is established.

Is the corporate world listening?

Balance or Burn Out   51

THERE IS no third choice.

I am a lay counsellor. Recently, while taking a leisurely stroll, I mulled over the cases my colleagues and I handled. There was a common thread that bound the varied patients that we counselled. It struck me then, that most professionals who came to see us could be classified as cases of burnouts—due to unbridled ambition, to a very strong need to dominate work relationships, to excessive stress and anxiety, or to unhealthy competition with peers. *She is fairer, he is smarter, they are richer* . . . not realizing, that any sort of comparison, including with oneself, is a sure source of tension.

Another fact that became clear to me was that in most cases, there was a *brown out* before the burnout (a common term for this is depression), a kind of warning signal, which was largely ignored by most people; the third common element in these cases appeared to be the lack of balance in life.

Most managers, for example, made no mention of regular exercise in their schedule. There was either no time, or inclination for even a brisk walk, much less a workout at a gym, suggesting a total lack of balance. Only a few mentioned having any worthwhile hobby. It was the work, their boss, or wives and children who were the focus in their lives. In fact, they found it painful when they became the focus of attention instead.

The renowned psychologist, Samuel Klarreich, in his book *The Stress Solution and Personal Effectiveness*, says:

> *Burnout is the depletion of your resources, both physical and emotional, caused by compulsive desire to achieve, due to exaggerated expectations, which you feel, must be fulfilled and which are typically, but are always, job related. Once these are not fulfilled, there is an overwhelming tendency towards cynicism, pessimism and negativity.*

Stephen Covey, in *The Seven Habits of Highly Effective People,* adds that, 'There is no real excellence in this world, which can be separated from right living.' Meaning, that excellence in life is not divisible. Excellence cannot be segmented or compartmentalised. If you are a workaholic and high achiever at work, it will eventually be at the cost of something else—poor health, or indifferent relationships.

What then is balanced living? A wise person will say that there are four elements of balanced living—spiritual, mental, physical and social. There are also different ways to help visualise the concept of balance. Ben Kubbasek has described balance succinctly: 'For me the old scale of justice helps. The base being your spiritual dimension, the pivot being our mental capacity, one arm being our physical condition and the other arm being our social life'.

Stephen Covey calls these elements the 'four dimensions of renewal'. At the macro level, the physical dimension would include exercise, nutrition and stress management. Social or emotional factors would refer to service, empathy, and intrinsic security. In the spiritual dimension, Covey includes value clarification, commitment, study and meditation, and mental will, spread across reading, visualising, planning, and writing.

To understand fully what these four dimensions are all about requires going into some detail. The questions asked in the physical dimension that need to be addressed may include whether we are eating the right kind of foods; and are we getting sufficient rest and relaxation, in addition to exercising on a regular basis? Most executives fail this test. The oft-repeated reason for not exercising is the lack of time. Physical fitness experts tell us that four hours a week is all that we require to stay fit. That represents a minuscule 2.3 per cent of the total exercise time in a week, with an assured return on the time invested.

Social balance normally occurs when life is lived in a win-win relationship within the family, friends, customers, suppliers and all other stakeholders of our lives. Win-lose or lose-wins are only temporary expedients, which extract a much greater price in the future. The social dimension would mean authenticity in our relationship with others.

The spiritual dimension is at the core of it all—your commitment, your centre; in fact, your very existence. This applies to all of us, regardless of our station in life, whether we are rich or poor, executives or pensioners, housewives or working mothers. This attribute can best be described through the following two quotes. In the first, McKay, a religious leader, said: 'The greatest battles of life are fought out daily in the silent chambers of the soul'. Martin Luther King put it only slightly differently when he said, 'I have so much to do today, I will need to spend another hour on my knees'.

Reading and writing can be extremely satisfying and stimulating mental activities for some. Others experience mental growth through music, painting, theatre and other mind-absorbing, yet, relaxing pursuits. It is important for each one of us to find our own mental moorings.

It is clear that a balance can be achieved only when we deal with all four dimensions in a state of equilibrium. To neglect one will affect the other, and consequently there would be a loss of balance.

So, there is no third choice, except to find that balance or experience burnout. We have it in us to make that choice, or to leave it to the professional counsellors to discover it for us.

Good People do Good Business 52

O UT OF the many new year resolutions my wife makes every year, two of these remain unimplemented year after year. They are:

1. I will not buy any more saris until I have used, at least once, all of the previous stock.
2. I will lose 3 kg.

This year, fortunately for us, she kept resolution number one for a decent period of six months and we generated some surplus to invest to stave off the ever-declining standard of living. What with low rates of interest, life is getting a bit difficult, particularly for those who like a tot or two in the evening,

I called our broker to bring the forms of all the mutual fund companies he dealt with. At the end of it, I picked three for investment purposes and left out the other seven. Almost all ten had demonstrated similar rates of return.

After the broker left, my wife asked me why I had given preference to the selected three over the others. I said, 'Somehow, I feel good about them'. It is the feel-good factor, everything else being equal, that determines why we choose one and not the other.

Let me give you another instance. If it were not for the take-away food options that are now available in Bangalore, the quality of food in our home, to use a cliché, would leave much to be desired. I called up my favourite *dhaba* and told the owner to send me three varieties of food on his menu. For reasons already mentioned, I have to deal with him on a regular basis. Two of the food items he sent were total flops. I rang him and told him in *shudh* Punjabi what I thought of his performance, and not one to waste a golden opportunity, I said, 'Gautam, *agar aisa khana khana thaa, to ghar ka khana kha lete*'. He heard me out, apologised profusely and hung up.

The next day, Gautam turned up in his car to personally deliver a free replacement for the poor quality meal of the day before. While making the delivery, he apologised again for the lapse. What was Gautam doing? He was establishing a feel-good factor between me (the client) and himself (the supplier). Gautam will always stay at the top of my list when I want to eat north Indian food.

It is not good enough today to be good. You need to build goodwill in your customers' minds, that your company is in the top two or three in their recall. Let me put it another way. You can be the best in your business but at that moment of reckoning, if I don't recall your name, you are not much use to me as a supplier.

Max DePree, the famous author of *Leadership Is An Art*, calls this feel-good factor as the intimacy of relationships. He goes on to say that intimacy is the heart of competence. It has to do with understanding, with believing, and with practice. It has to do with the relationship to one's work.

How does one develop intimacy? One cannot do a bullet presentation on a soft skill like intimacy. It cannot be understood by a formula, nor mandated from the top but it can certainly be created. Therefore, I can best explain it with folklore:

An American couple goes to a store in Tokyo to buy some electrical goods. As they are packing for their departure back to the US on the following day, the husband decides to check out the gadget and finds to his dismay that it is not working. It is well past the store's closing time and he is upset that it was a total waste of time and money to have bought the Japanese gadget. As the husband and wife are still talking about their deep disappointment, they hear the doorbell ring and open the door to find a Japanese gentleman in a suit, with a steward wearing white gloves and carrying a box.

The manager explains that one of the unserviceable pieces left aside had been mixed up with the rest of the inventory. The moment they discovered their fault, the manager wanted to make an immediate replacement.

But where do they find their American visitor? He could be anywhere in Tokyo. Only a driven manager, who feels good about the organisation, would do what this manager did. He immediately got in touch with the credit card company of his customer and through their help, got his American address. The person who picked up the telephone gave the manager the name of the hotel the customer was staying at.

And there he was in person with a bunch of flowers for the lady and the replacement, as well as a sincere apology. How would you feel if you were that customer? You would tell this story in drawing-room conversations when the question of good service cropped up.

How would you feel if you were working in such a company? You would instinctively know how a wrong done to the customer needs to redressed. No formal procedure or guidelines will be needed to guide you. This way of dealing with the situation will become an unwritten covenant of the company. Such covenants induce freedom of action in the employees, rather than the paralysis caused by rules on How to Deal with Warranty claims.

As I said earlier, you can't look for tips for building feel-good factors in your organisation. Let me illustrate this phenomenon in another way. I once worked for a large industrial group. Our group chairman was a doyen of industry in the 1980s. The senior executives of the group met in Goa every year for the annual review meetings. That was the structured side of work with guest speakers and all that normally goes on during an annual conference.

But on a couple of evenings during our stay, we would gather around the chairman. He would tell us nostalgically about how he developed business in west Asia, how he found this collaborator or the other, how he made friends in Egypt and how he once accepted a large consignment of dates from Iran because that was the only way the customer could pay for the engineering equipment our group had supplied.

His senior colleagues would fill in some missing details that the chairman had forgotten, or remind him of some dinner that they all had with a dealer in Jaipur, when they were served spicy Rajasthani food.

There were no management *fundas* discussed during those evenings. It was more like a tribal chief talking to his tribe around the log fire. It helped to create a sense of history for us, for our group and what we were all about. We felt good about the group and about ourselves, and a silent process of bonding and intimacy between us took place.

And that reflected in our interactions and in our dealings when we went back to our respective jobs. We were friends doing business together and not mere colleagues who happened to belong to a large industrial group. We were not there to be 'one up' on the other. The thought of short-changing someone else was, if at all, a rare phenomenon.

There is a danger to intimacy from the superficial, the over-ambitious, the clear-cut concept types, the legal contract or the 'I want a clear-cut approach to this, people' and 'the legal contract, people?' Therefore, it is always in danger of extinction. The leader has to be watchful for such attacks on intimacy.

Alexander Solzhenitsyn, speaking to the graduating class at Harvard, said this about legalistic relationships: 'Society based on the letter of the law and never reaching any higher fails to take advantage of the full range of human possibilities. The letter of the law is too cold and formal to have a beneficial influence on society. Whenever the tissue of life is woven of legalistic relationships this creates an atmosphere of spiritual mediocrity that paralyses men's noblest impulse.'

Companies are nothing but societies. Companies that promote a legalistic structure somehow stay stuck in the rut of mediocrity. The pity is that they don't realise it because they have not experienced the option intimacy provides.

It is all about the personal chemistry between people in the organisation and the feel-good factor between them that builds big business.

Would it be an exaggeration if I were to say that only good people can do good business and sell good goods?

Index